The First Time Parent's Baby Manual

By: Clifford Dale James III, BS, MD, FAAP

(This book is just an excuse for me to write my name
with all those silly initials behind it.)

D1564133

First published by Dog Ear Publishing
4011 Vincennes Rd
Indianapolis, IN 46268
www.dogearpublishing.net

ISBN: 978-1-4575-4217-6

This book is printed on acid-free paper.

Printed in the United States of America

Although the wardrobe is comfortable, I am often mistaken for the plumber, maintenance man or dog walker.

My favorite quote: Everyone is here as an example, some of us are just the bad examples.

Dedication

This book is dedicated to:

God: He never gave up on me even when I gave up on him.

Dalton James: My first son and the best pediatric teacher I've ever had.

Tyler Scott: My step-son, thanks for continuing my education and teaching me; when you go from one child to two you go from being a parent to a referee.

Kaden James: Our brand new baby boy who is helping me write this book. He is so smart.

Mom and Dad: Thanks for believing in me and loving me in spite of myself.

Kristi Roberson James: You are a great wife, an amazing friend and thanks for listening to me dream and brainstorm this book. Thanks for not divorcing me when I come up with things to do that take time away from our family.

My patients: The parents and children with whom I have had the opportunity to be involved with and watch grow up; you made me the doctor I am today.

Dr. Ben Brouhard: My department head in residency who allowed me to get away with a lot in order for me to be the doctor I am today.

Mountain Dew: The ambrosia of the gods and the energy that keeps me going.

My office staff: Sue Gray, Michele Hall, MaryAnn Newman, Melissa Maupin, Tonya Thomas, Kesha Dryman, Amanda Moore, and Ashley Powell; you guys make my job easy and make me look better than I ever could by myself.

Grandma: She told me as a little boy I'd grow up to be a pediatrician.

Red: He was a good dog.

Useless information books: Because knowing how big an ostrich's eye is in relation to its brain is important for a pediatrician to know.

Table of Contents

Introduction

**Congratulations Mr. and Mrs. Smith!
Here is your baby and his owner's manuals.**

I've often been asked, "Why don't babies come with a how to manual?" After years of answering the same question, I thought it would be a good idea to create a book specifically written with new parents in mind.

This book is not meant to replace your child's doctor. It is meant to give parents a resource to save you time, money, and stress. If you read the entire book it will answer the most common questions new parents ask. The book is intended to make it easier to understand what your doctor means and why they say the things they do. It will hopefully also bring a little lightheartedness to parenthood. Remember when you were a kid and you swore you were going "to be cool" and not as uptight as your parents? Being a parent can be fun. It's best to enjoy parenting as it happens instead of just looking back at it fondly when it is all over.

Many parenting books can be too complicated, boring, or misleading to new parents. When I was preparing to be a first-time parent and read the parenting books, I had difficulty even as a pediatrician finishing reading any of the books from start to finish. I would have rather pulled my own teeth out than read what seemed more like a textbook or owner's manual for a computer. Some of the books were so lengthy that by the time I would have gotten the entire thing read my kid would be graduating from high school. Often the books also seemed to mislead parents by putting things in very black and white terms, when in reality there is a large variation in the normal development of each child. This book is designed to help first-time parents who know very little about caring for babies, nor much about medical care. It contains all the details I would share with you if I had unlimited time to teach you about your child. This is not intended to be an all-inclusive pediatric textbook but merely a parent's guide. There are numerous ways to properly care for your baby. The information contained here is based on my successful experience as a pediatrician and father; however, your pediatrician may have medically sound recommendations not contained within this book.

If you are reading this book you are either a parent or about to become one. Congratulations! Enjoy every minute. Babies do not stay young for very long. Remember new parenthood comes with lots of mistakes. Mistakes do not make you a bad parent and these happen to all of us. As we go through this book together, I will share some dumb things I have done along the way. Just remember that even the people who wrote the boring books about parenting have screwed things up too. I sure would like to see how their kids turned out ... since they are so smart. Throughout the book you will find "Kaden's" thoughts or logs. These show what was going on in our house while various developmental stages were happening.

Chapter 1

Finding a pediatrician

"Honey, are you sure this is the best way to find a pediatrician?"

Choosing a pediatrician can be a very stressful decision-making process. This relationship is long-term and establishing a rapport with this physician will be important to your child's well being. Given the importance of this decision, what is the best way to find a good pediatrician? There is always the blind folded Yellow Pages advertisement selection, the quarter toss, or the office you drive by on the way to work. However, many parents will want to make a more informed decision.

First, make a list of possible pediatricians in your area. A good place to start is with the list of providers that accept your health insurance. Your health insurance company can provide this list and it will be sure to tick you off, since the company will limit your options of pediatricians. Most people find having someone from a far-off office control who you can select as a pediatrician incites some frustration and anger. Your pediatrician list can be found in your health provider's book, website or by calling their customer service line. Keep their number easily accessible; you may want to call it later to yell at them when you get your hospital bill!

Take this list of pediatricians, to your friends and acquaintances who have children and ask who they recommend. They may be able to give you a good idea about the doctor's community reputation and/or the type of care they provide. The doctor's reputation is formed by their personality and rapport with patients and families. Ask what they are like as a person. There are many great doctors but not all will fit with your personality. I am the first to admit I am not the doctor for everybody; you will either love me or hate me based on my personality. Ask your friends if they think YOU would like a particular doctor they can recommend.

Ask your obstetrician as well as the nursery staff at the hospital where you will be delivering your baby who they recommend. You should ask these questions well in advance of your due date. This will give you an idea about the pediatrician's professional reputation and medical skills. Their opinion may be one of the most valuable because they are able to compare all the doctors in the area. There are numerous find-a-doctor websites or phone numbers, but don't rely on them as a reliable resource as they are typically paid advertisements and are biased.

Various other websites can also provide information about a doctor's history of medical lawsuits, parental/patient feedback, and cost comparisons. Some of these websites may charge you for the information but you can find out similar information through your insurance company. There are also free physician ranking websites that provide patient comments about doctors and/or practices.

Finally, when you have your list narrowed down, schedule an appointment with some of the pediatric practices to conduct a "prenatal visit" to interview the doctor. Most practices will do a prenatal visit for free or for a nominal fee. This will give you a better idea of which practice will fit you and your family best. For your baby to receive the best medical care, you will need to feel comfortable with the pediatrician and their staff.

The following is fundamental information you should seek during the prenatal visit:

1. **Are they board certified?** This tells you the pediatrician completed an American Academy of Pediatric certified residency and passed a very comprehensive medical board exam. The American Academy of Pediatrics mandates a minimum number of continuing medical education hours annually and requires retesting every 10 years. If they are not board certified, chances are they have been unable to pass the test or were too lazy to study for the exam.

2. **How will they answer your questions when you call the office?** If you call the office and ask a question, what happens? Many offices throughout the country have started charging to answer questions. Find out if the office does this and what the cost is. Also find out the time frame in which your calls will be returned and who will make them. There are many acceptable ways this can be done, but it is nice to know before you have a critical medical question related to your baby.

3. **Where do they have medical privileges?** This is the hospital where they will admit patients. Ask if they see their patients in the hospital or if someone else follows their patients. Many hospitals use a hospitalist pediatrician who is only responsible for patients in the hospital. In many ways this is better, since the doctors who care for your sick child are always in the hospital and not trying to cover a busy office at the same time.

4. **What are their office hours?** You will need to ensure their office hours are compatible with your schedule. Large multi-physician practices may offer more flexible hours and weekend coverage, but you might see different doctors each time. Small

practice office schedules may have less flexibility, but you will see the same doctor almost all the time. There are pros and cons of each type of practice to consider in your decision. Decide what balance is the most important for your family.

5.   **What is their policy regarding sick visits?** If your little one is sick you won't want to wait several days before being seen. Most pediatricians know this and will usually see babies the day you call. There are exceptions to this though. I would urge you to call promptly as soon as you know your baby is sick. This allows the office to give you advice, ensure the child is seen as needed, and allows for any needed testing. It is best to know the policy before the need for your first sick visit arises.

6.   **Plan to ask the doctor a weird question most people would not think of asking.** This may simply be something you personally want to know but the idea is to get them to think on their feet. Most parents ask similar questions and pediatricians have practiced answers for them. Be creative. Think of a memorable question. This will begin building rapport between you and the doctor. The strangest question I've been asked was, "What is your mission statement?"[1]

7.   **If you believe in something different than the norm ask the doctor how they feel about it.** If you have a religious belief preventing vaccination or using blood products, you need to know if the doctor will be supportive of them. If the pediatrician cannot be supportive of your beliefs, this may not be a good fit for your family.

After all your office interviews, you should have an idea of where your family will best fit. After you have chosen your doctor, find out what you need to do to get your child into the practice. Every practice has different policies regarding new patients.

I recommend you make a list of all your questions for each visit. Ask your questions at the beginning of the visit, ensuring all your concerns are addressed. Never withhold a question just because you thought it was dumb or not important. The only dumb question is the one you did not ask. It is

---

[1] If you are wondering what my mission statement is, it states: "We will try to treat each child as if they were our own, offering high quality health care while simultaneously crushing the competition and taking over the world." (I had to have something for the bank and I thought it sounded funny).

the doctor's job to figure out how important it is, and anything worrying you is worth the time to answer.

Kaden's recommendations:

As the baby I would like to add my top 10 recommendations you may not have thought of as the parent:

1. The pediatrician should have warm hands. Trust me this is important as I will have to get naked in their office, and I should at least be touched by warm hands.

2. Make sure the office doesn't smell like poop. It is bad enough that I have to smell my own poop, but I sure don't want to smell someone else's dirty diaper too.

3. Ask if they have emergency diapers and wipes. If my parents forget the diaper bag I don't want to have to be sitting in my own nastiness.

4. Along the same line as number three, do they have formula or bottles handy? This way if my parents are really forgetful I won't have to starve to death.

5. Is the office cool looking? I like bright colors so please don't take me to a boring looking office.

6. Are there toys for me to play with while we are in the office? I tend to get in less trouble if I have something to do other than drive my parents crazy.

7. Is the doctor fun? I am going to have to listen to them talk for the next 18 years so it would be nice if they are fun to be around.

8. Will the doctor hurt me? I am going to get scared somewhere along the line while they are caring for me. Will they take their time and try to help me or are they going to be in a hurry and hurt me trying to examine me?

9. Would you trust them with your life? If you can't trust them with your life then don't trust them with mine.

10. Do they have warm hands? Yes I know this is the same as number one, but it is the most important to me.

Chapter 2

Paying for this book both in time and money

Don't think of a baby as the end of all your dreams...
except of course those dreams!

I am sure you have already found out babies are an expensive proposition. Walk into any baby store and you will find multiple aisles of endless gadgets that the retail market is sure you and your baby cannot live without. But don't worry, I will prioritize things you really need, make suggestions how to buy less expensive items, and generally make preparing for a baby far less painful. The cheaper alternative truly would have been to have a midlife crisis, buy a red convertible, and travel around the world; however, you have chosen parenthood. With that in mind, we will try and make the best of this decision.

Do not start off buying tons of formula before your baby arrives. Many parents want to stockpile large amounts because they know they will need formula and that it would be nice to have a "paid" stash of this expensive stuff before the tike comes. The kicker is that a baby's formula can get changed multiple times during the first two weeks of life for various medical reasons and many stores will not let you return it for safety reasons. Therefore, you could be stuck with expensive formula you won't be able to use. The hospital will start your baby on a formula in the hospital and they will usually send you home with a couple of day's worth. Buy just a few days worth at a time for the first week or two. After you get through the first two weeks, the chances that your baby's formula will change becomes less likely and then it makes sense to buy more at a time. When you go to your doctor's visit, ask if they have formula samples or coupons. Most medical offices receive these for free from the formula representatives and usually have no problem giving them to you. The pediatricians will not always think to give you samples; however you should not hesitate to ask for it. The formula company's website will also have substantial money saving coupons. Over a year these coupons can add up to a significant amount of money.

Do not make large investments in diapers before the baby arrives nor should you ask for diapers at showers. You won't know your baby's skin sensitivity prior to delivery. In the diaper business, the most expensive brand is not always the best. I have had more diaper rashes and allergies from brand name diapers than generic brands. Diapers are not a fashion statement and are only there to catch pee and poop so spend as little money on them as possible.

Cloth diapers are also an option. Cloth diapers can save you about $900-1600 per baby after you recover from the initial investment and even with the associated laundry costs. It cannot be argued cloth diapers are better for the environment and they do cause less diaper rashes. If you choose to use them, I am sure Mother Nature will be very happy and you are not doing any harm to your baby. Cloth diapers could be an exception to the baby shower rule, so ask for lots of these at your shower.

Do not spend a small fortune on diaper creams. The active ingredient in most diaper rash cream is zinc oxide so just buy the cheapest one you can find. The real secret to treating a diaper rash is never let the rash develop in the first place. Most rashes are caused by not changing the baby's diaper often enough, so check their diaper frequently. If you use diaper rash cream every time, it should prevent the diaper rash from ever starting.

There are many products for cleaning your baby. What do they do and why do you need them? There is baby shampoo, which is to clean your baby's hair. You will find the most important selling point is whether it causes tears or not. In all honesty though, water in their eyes causes tears. Just be careful to protect their eyes when you are washing their hair as whatever type used can make them cry. Any baby shampoo is fine, so save some money. Baby lotions are more about making your baby smell like a baby and not dirty diapers and spit-up milk. Find one you like the smell of and pay what you can afford. If your baby has any skin rashes, your doctor won't recommend baby lotions. Baby powder is also just for smell and serves no other function. Many pediatricians no longer recommend using it due to the risk of getting the powder into the baby's lungs. If you do use baby powder, dust it into the diaper away from the baby before putting it on the baby.

Many people never use changing tables and just change the diaper wherever the diaper and baby happen to be. This may be on the floor, couch, lap, counter, bed…any place except a changing table. If you get the baby home and think it would be easier to change them with a changing table, then by all means go and buy one.

Now, I am sure there are at least a hundred different varieties of baby bottles out there! All of these bottles have some slight variation and are marketed with the premise that your baby would be better off "using this bottle" over another one. The advertised difference between different types of bottles is usually "a bunch of hooey". Start off with the cheapest bottle you can find and it will likely be the one you use at least 90 percent of the time. If your baby has a hard time drinking from it, then at least you haven't invested a lot of money in something you have to change. Some bottles cost as much as $8-$12 each and don't work any better than the cheaper versions. Some expensive models also require an engineering degree to take apart to wash and get back together. Nipples for bottles are the same. Use the cheapest nipple in the slow to medium flow and it will work for almost all the babies. If you have problems, then start looking for something different and more expensive. Here is one of those time-saving tidbits: You do NOT ever need to boil your bottles or nipples, even if your mom says you are supposed to. You need to wash them in hot soapy water. Your dishwasher can more than adequately clean your baby's bottles. Your doctor may have you boil pacifiers or nipples if your baby gets thrush, but only while the thrush is being treated.

Bottled water is expensive and is no better to mix your formula with than tap water. Most of the bottled water actually comes from PWS, which stands for public water supply. Most bottled water filters out fluoride, which is needed for strong teeth and to prevent dental caries I recommend you use city water that has been fluoridated. If you do not have a safe water source, make sure you buy nursery water, which is fluoridated bottled water. Lastly, contrary to what your mom or grandmother says, you do not have to boil the water from the tap to mix your formula. The only exception would be if you knew your water source was contaminated due to flooding or something else. It will not do any harm to boil the water, but it is sure going to waste a lot of your time.

Babies grow extremely fast and if you do not have a lot of extra money lying around you may want to skip the extra expense of a bassinet. These are nice to have those first couple of months when the baby is waking up frequently during the night for feedings and other things. It allows you to keep the baby close but the baby will outgrow it very quickly and it would be cheaper to just put the baby bed in your room for the first couple of months and then move it to the nursery later. Similarly, those little, soft, bumper pads are very cute in the baby bed, but that is all they are—cute. When a baby actually starts to move around your pediatrician will recommend removing them because they can become a safety hazard—more money better spent somewhere else.

The following is a list of commonly purchased items that are usually never used or are retired very quickly:

Diaper pails: a place to put used diapers is a must, but fancy pails with special insert type bags are a pain (hard to change the bags and smell awful when you do).

Bottle warmers: These take too long and did you know you do not really need to warm milk? You condition a baby to the temperature of milk. They will like the temperature you get them used to over time. I recommend room temperature. I trained my little guy to drink his formula straight out of the fridge. When I started taking him to daycare he would throw up all day long. One day I walked in early and saw them warming his bottle. The warm milk was why he was throwing up. He was used to having his formula cold and the warm temperature upset his belly.

Diaper wipe warmer: The idea of using these is nice and sounds comfortable, but the warmer never seems to be where you are. If you are going to only change diapers at a designated changing table, this might be a product you would use on a regular basis.

Fancy thermometers: You could spend a large sum of money on fancy thermometers and gadgets to take temperatures, which are usually pieces of junk. We recommend you buy a digital axillary thermometer. If you spent more than $8-$10 on it, you were robbed. Some doctors still want rectal temperatures. Ask your pediatrician which they prefer. If you spend enough money on one of the temporal thermometers, these are amazing and reliable. But cheap forehead scanners, pacifier thermometers, and most tympanic thermometers (ear thermometers) are a waste of your money.

Some things are worth their weight in gold:

Changing pad kits: These are little kits that will have a little container of wipes, a changing pad, and enough room to store a diaper or two.

Baby sacks: These are little gown things that cinch at the bottom around the baby's feet. They are great for newborns and allow easy access to your baby for frequent diaper changing.

Baby monitors: These allow you to leave your little angel while they are sleeping and get something done somewhere else in the house...or get a little nap yourself.

10 second thermometers: The time it takes to take a baby's temperature with a normal thermometer is about the same time it takes for a pregnancy test to run and both feel like forever. Make it as short as possible.

Tylenol: Your little bundle of joy is going to give you a headache or two. Take two and call someone in the morning.

Self-closing pacifier: Your little baby will spit out his/her pacifier accidentally or on purpose. To prevent washing it a hundred times a day use these instead—an amazing invention.

Hand-me-downs: If you know someone who will give you things you need to take care of your little person consider him or her a Godsend. Just be careful to look on the Internet as toys and strollers may have had a recall for being unsafe. Car seats should not be used second hand as they may have expired or been in a wreck that makes them unsafe for your baby.

**While writing this book and editing it my wife Kristi and I found we are expecting a little baby boy. We have bought all the things I highly recommend. She has also bought the wipe warmer, changing table, diaper pail and bumper pad that I wrote were a waste of money. This shows that one person's trash is another's treasure, even in the same house.

Kaden's recommendations: As a baby I'm not really worried about costs and saving money. Here is a list of my recommendations:

1. I really like my vibrating chair. Mine is like a lamb and it feels really warm and cozy.

2. My Daddy's ideas about the diaper wipe warmer are all crazy. I personally like it very much and wish I had a diaper and clothing warmer.

3. I think those baby sacks are silly and it makes me look like I'm wearing a dress.

4. I prefer to throw my pacifier and make my parents play fetch.

5. Forget all the politically correct stuff, you do want to know what my parents used on me don't you? I have Pampers Swaddler diapers, Avent bottles, drink Enfamil Gentlease formula as well as breast milk. I have a monitor my parents barely use, an exergen forehead scanning thermometer and a DeKor diaper pail.

6. I have many toys my parents have bought for me, but my favorite things to play with are my parents' cell phones, keys, boxes and outlet covers.

7. Baby proof me all you like—it just gives me a challenge and goal for the day.

8. Always give yourself an extra 15 minutes to get ready to go anywhere since I guarantee you may need to feed me, change

my diaper or your own clothes and look for the keys I've hidden from you (this happens to my mommy often).

9. Do not feel like a failure if your life as a parent does not look the same as the dream you had of being a parent. It is harder to take care of me than you ever imagined but I am more awesome than you could have ever dreamed.

10. As you are crying yourself to sleep just remember I love you and you are the best parent I have ever had.

Chapter 3
Newborn plumbing

Some joys of parenting were not in the brochure.

Not all babies are created equal. Some are girls and some are boys and their plumbing is completely different. Chances are you have had some encounters with the different parts of the two sexes (after all you did just have a baby), but you are going to see some things people probably did not warn you about. This is where having this manual comes in handy.

Since my mom always said ladies first, we will start off with the girls and a little anatomy lesson.

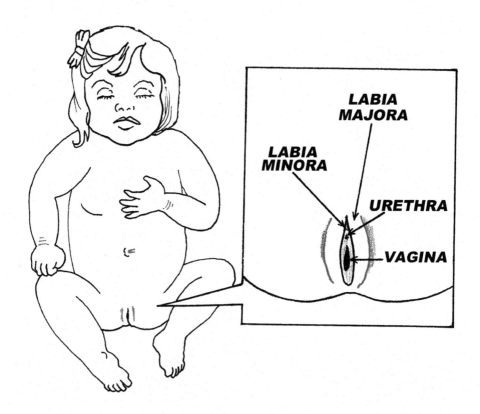

The plumbing section is here because it generates questions like: What is that? Is that normal? How do I need to take care of things down there? We will start with some of the variations you can see right after the baby is born. Depending on how close you were to her due date the external genitalia may look very different. The closer the baby is to her due date the larger the labia majora will be. If a baby is very immature, she may look wide open and her labia minora looks bigger than the labia majora. This is completely normal and as the baby gets older the labia majora will fill out and get bigger. In its full term state the labia majora should be bigger and completely cover the labia minora. The labia minora is a lot more tender type of skin. If it is exposed you need to be more gentle when you clean it than you would with the labia majora, which is covered with normal outside skin. Newborn babies may have vaginal mucosal tags. These are little flaps of skin—little extra pieces of the vaginal type skin that vary in size—that you may see coming out of the vagina. These are influenced by mom's hormones and after the baby is born will shrink and go away. You have to be gentle as you wipe them because they are more sensitive. In rare cases a baby's hymen may be completely closed off and you will see a white-colored, bulging sack coming out of the vaginal opening. If you see this you need to ask your pediatrician because it will need to be surgically corrected.

When you are wiping a little girl's bottom you will find that poop will go everywhere and make quite a mess. You have to clean all poop out of the vaginal area just like you do off her bottom. Always wipe her vagina from front to back to make sure that you are not wiping poop into the vaginal area. This is the way little girls should always wipe to keep from getting vaginal irritation, urinary tract infections or yeast infections.

As Mom's hormones were high while she was pregnant some of these will be passed to the baby girl. Because of these hormones, the first several days of life you may see a white mucous discharge come out of her vagina. This is completely normal and you just need to gently wipe it away when you change her diaper. It is also not unusual to see trace amounts of bright red blood on days 2-5 of life. This is also from mom's hormones and it is kind of like having a little period. Again just gently wipe it away when changing diapers. It can last a day or two and seems a little more common in babies who are breastfeeding, which makes sense when you consider more of mom's hormones come from the milk.

Some problems or questions you may have about your baby's vagina:

By far the most common problem that is going to happen down here is a diaper rash. The most common type of rash is just an irritated, contact rash either from being sensitive to a type of diaper (in this case the whole diaper area is involved) or to staying wet or dirty for too long (just the area that was wet or dirty will be irritated). These rashes will be anywhere from slightly to extremely red and you want to treat it with a diaper rash cream that contains zinc oxide.

The next most common rash is a yeast infection. Yeast is not really an infection; it is more of an overgrowth. It likes to grow in wet areas, like diapers, where there is no competition (after being on antibiotics and the bacteria on the skin is killed off). This rash will be bright red and usually have bright red little dots around the edges. Yeast infection type rashes will need a prescription ointment to treat them (I usually advise treating until the rash is gone and then for three additional days). Another problem that little girls can have down here is called labial adhesions. This is usually due to bad diaper rashes or to not getting the area good and clean. Labial adhesions are where the two opposing surfaces of the labia minora become irritated and fuse. In its most extensive state the labia minora can completely fuse shut where there is barely a hole for urine to exit the urethra, much less flow properly. This can set your baby up for a urinary tract infection. Make sure you are cleaning your baby well every day and if you see that her opening is closing up be sure to let your doctor know and they will fix the problem.

Another common question parents have is why are they rubbing up against things or wanting to play with themselves down there? Did someone do something to them or is something bothering them? First make sure she does not have a rash, because yeast infections can itch, but usually this is just a normal activity. They figure out that it feels good to them and they will try to do it all the time in some of the most embarrassing places. I knew one little girl that would rub herself against the divider of the shopping cart at stores looking very happy while her parents watched mortified. Just try to ignore them and the behavior will eventually go away. They do like to stick things in their vagina too so if you notice a foul smell down there (different from the smell of poop) see your doctor because they probably have something like toilet paper stuck up there and it can lead to an infection.

People have a terrible time saying the word vagina. When vagina is too embarrassing to say they come up with some of the stupidest things I have ever heard that seem a lot more embarrassing. Here are a few examples that I have heard over the years.

Kitty cat

Muffin

Biscuit

Monkey

Coochee

Cushion

Hot dog bun

Va Jay Jay

Waa Yaa Yaa

Moo Cat

Hoo Yaa (I'm not 100 percent sure of this spelling)

Hoo Ha

Cooch

Cha Cha

Cooter

Tooter

Toot Toot

Kaden's Comments: I am not allowed to comment on this section. My parents won't even let me look at the words much less the picture. I am convinced that the way you tell the difference from the boys and the girls is we have blue socks and they have pink socks.

Now for the little boy's anatomy lesson:

We should start this little section off with one of the questions that will be asked before the baby is even born; to circumcise or leave uncircumcised? This seems to generate very heated debates so let me try to put this in as unbiased terms as possible. Medical studies have found that circumcised males have less penile cancer, less problems with phymosis (a condition in which the foreskin cannot be retracted to expose the glans), and less sexually transmitted disease. With that being said, the differences are minor and more a way of medically justifying circumcision. On the other side of the argument circumcision comes with some pain and some surgical risks. It is also felt that uncircumcised penises have greater sensitivity of the glans

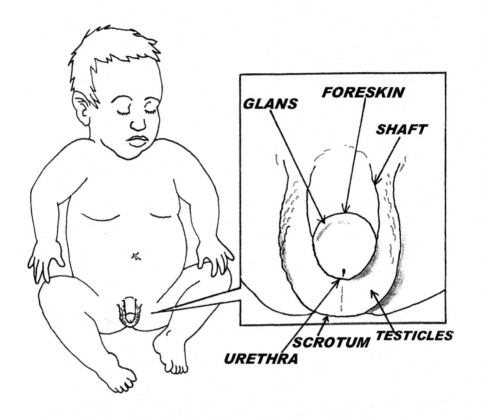

during sexual stimulation. So what do you do? Here is my advice on the matter. Circumcision is mainly a cultural and social exercise. If everyone that your child is going to be around has had it done then it can be socially troubling to them to be different (yes they will look). It's also something that can be a big deal socially when they get older and are in gym showers or dating. This seems to vary culturally as well as geographically. I recommend you do whatever you feel comfortable with and feel is in the best interest of your little boy. Both have been done for centuries (I am pretty sure uncircumcised was around first), and boys have been thriving either way.

With that out of the way, how do you take care of each type of penis? The point of a circumcision is to cut away the excess foreskin and expose the glans (head of the penis). A newborn penis will have adhesions that have stuck the foreskin to the head of the glans. When your little guy comes back from having his circumcision done, the penis will usually be wrapped in gauze covered in Vaseline and you will see a little bloodstaining. The gauze usually falls off or is removed after the first day and you will see a bright red and very raw looking glans. The main thing you need to do at this stage is put some petroleum jelly (trust me I really wanted to use the brand name) on the head of the penis as well as the front of the diaper. This keeps the penis from sticking to the diaper. On about the second day the head of the penis will appear to be covered in a yellow, gooey-looking mucous. This is not a sign of infection but is just the way a circumcision heals. When the yellow goo disappears about 3-5 days after the circumcision, it means the penis is healed and you do not have to use the petroleum jelly anymore.

A circumcised penis is not a maintenance-free penis. As a boy gets a little chunkier in the first couple months of life he will develop a little fat pad right above the penis that will sometimes push the foreskin over the glans of the penis. You will need to gently retract this every time you change his diaper. If you do not do this then the foreskin and glans will get irritated from urine and rubbing and will begin to stick together and form a foreskin adhesion. These will have to be lysed by your doctor and can get so bad that he could have a revision of his circumcision. Make sure that you pull it back till you see the lip along the edge of the glans every time you change their diaper to prevent this from happening. You will usually have to do this as long as he has the fat pad pushing the fore-skin down, which is usually until 18-24 months of age.

The uncircumcised penis has to be taken care of a little differently. You may hear varying tales of what you have to do if a little boy is uncircum-cised, but really you just want to leave it alone. You need to wash the out-side skin just like you wash the rest of his body, but you need to leave everything else alone. The foreskin is usually stuck to the glans of the penis when a baby is born and if you try to pull it back you will cause trauma that will not only hurt but can lead to scarring. When a little one is one to two years old the adhesions will usually start to loosen up so you can try to gen-tly retract the foreskin back and clean the glans gently with water. If it does not loosen up that is fine and it may not happen until a boy gets to be 10 and puberty starts to kick in. You may see some white gooey stuff come out of the hole in the foreskin occasionally. This is called smegma and is just dead skin that is sloughing off the foreskin and glans and has nowhere to go except out the little hole. If this smegma is accumulating under the foreskin you may see small whitish yellow bumps under the skin at the tip of the penis. These will eventually work themselves out the hole and are nothing to worry about.

Some problems or questions you may have about your baby's penis:

Hydrocele- You may notice that one or both of your little guy's testicles look huge. This is usually a hydrocele. A hydrocele is a collection of fluid around the testicle itself and forms from a small connection to the abdominal cavity through the inguinal canal. This will usually resolve by the time the little guy is one year old. If it does not then surgery may be required to repair it, but luckily this is rare. Your pediatrician may diagnose this by holding a light to the scrotum to see if the light will shine through. If the light shows clearly through, it rules out any mass in the scrotum.

Undescended testicles- You may notice that your little man only has one testicle or no testicles in his scrotum. This is not an unusual thing especially in premature babies. Your pediatrician will try to find the testicles and most of the time the testicles are in the inguinal canal which is in the crease between the thigh and hip) and can be brought down with some gentle pressure. The testicles should be down in the scrotum by the time the baby is one year of age or surgery will have to be done to bring them down. Testicles that remain in the abdominal cavity past the year mark have a higher chance of developing testicular cancer and/or causing sterility.

Inguinal hernia- If you notice a third testicle, a big bulge in the scrotum, or a bulging mass in the groin area, this is an inguinal hernia. Inguinal hernias will always have to be surgically corrected. The surgery will have to happen sooner than later since the hernia can lead to intestinal obstruction.

Torsion of the testicle- If you have a baby boy that is screaming his bloody head off and one testicle is swollen and higher up than the other, it could be a torsion of the testicle. This occurs when the testicle twists and cuts off its own blood supply. This is a medical emergency and must be surgically corrected within the first several hours or the young man may lose that testicle. If you suspect torsion of the testicle get to an emergency room as soon as possible and do not allow them to put you off for hours. You need to be seen right away.

Vanishing penis- This is a frequent reason parents bring their little boy to see the doctor. In most cases the baby is usually kind of chunky and develops a fat pad above his penis. This fat pad can get so big that his penis retracts into it so you can no longer see it at all. This is usually nothing to worry about and as the little boy loses his baby fat the penis will start making a more regular appearance.

Diaper rashes- Baby boys get the same type of diaper rashes as little girls get. The most common is a simple irritated rash from staying wet or dirty too long or from a diaper rubbing the wrong way. These are easy taken care of with some liberal application of diaper rash cream. Little boys can also get yeast infection rashes. These will be bright red with little red dots around the edges and will need a prescription cream to clear it up.

Mystery pee- This is when a little boy pees and gets everything wet: you, his clothes, blanket and yet he and his diaper remain completely dry. Just a little tip: point his penis down when you put on the diaper. It will save you getting drenched with the mystery pee.

Masturbation- Parents are mortified that at a very early age little boys find out where their penis is and just cannot pay it enough attention. Just relax as this is very normal behavior on their part and anyone that has ever had a little boy will be glad to sympathize with you.

Here is a little funny story from my own personal experience. When my little boy was about four years old we were driving down the road and he said, "Daddy I wish my penis was purple." I asked him why and he replied, "I just like the color purple." A couple of days went by and he was taking a bath and he yelled, "Daddy, Daddy come here quick!" I ran as quickly as I could thinking that something had gone terribly wrong. When I got to the tub he proudly pointed to his penis and said, "Look Daddy my wish came true. My penis is purple." Just a little cold water can make a boy's day.

People evidently have a very hard time saying the word penis. Because of how bad penis sounds here are some of the interesting names I have heard it called over the years.

Worm

Bait and tackle

Peanut (this is the wonderful term my parents saddled me with; grade school was tough for the kid with a peanut)

Little snake

Wizzer

Pee pee

Willie

Bird

Wiener

Talley Whacker

Tadpole

The boys

Little wiggler

Kaden's Comments: My parents call my parts my penis. To be honest I would like it to have a cooler sounding name. I was thinking of something along the line of bronco or hurricane (and several branded names that could get me in trouble). I just like the fact that I can pee on stuff and make people scream.

CHAPTER 4

Feeding the monster

The calming ability of food is amazing.

W ell, we have a baby and they are going to eat. Hopefully you have given some thought to giving the little tike some food. We basically have two choices: breastfeeding and bottle-feeding. Which one of these two you choose depends on many factors. I am going to try to point out as impartially as possible, the pros and cons of each so you can make an informed decision that best suits your lifestyle.

Breastfeeding is the way Mother Nature intended babies to be fed and it has been proven for the entire time of man to be an effective way of feeding a baby. Over time we came up with substitutes for breast milk for various and assorted reasons. Here are the arguments.

Pros:

1. It is the natural way to feed your baby. Hard to argue with this logic, and I'm not even going to try.

2. It is cheaper than formula. This is a great reason to breastfeed. Formula is very expensive and will easily cost you thousands of dollars over the course of the baby's first year of life. Breastfeeding is essentially free of charge. If you also factor in the cost of bottles, dishwashing detergent, and time to prepare formula it gets even more expensive.

3. It is healthier for your baby. Scientifically this statement has been proven over time; breast milk is better digested and easier on babies' stomachs. They have fewer issues with constipation and reflux. Babies receive antibodies to diseases that Mom has had in the past passed to them through breast milk. These antibodies protect them until their own immune system starts to work at full capacity.

4. It is a great way to bond with your baby. Many moms that have done both bottle and breastfeeding state there is no comparison with the bond you develop with your baby when you produce their milk and provide all their needs. Moms giving their baby a bottle will bond with baby, but will miss out on this experience.

5. There are no bottles to wash since the baby is not using a bottle.

Cons:

1. Breastfeeding is time consuming as babies eat all the time. Their first couple of months they will eat every two to three hours and it may take them up to 45 minutes each time in the beginning. This means you will be feeding your baby up to six hours each day for the first month or two. As Mom is the only one able to breastfeed the baby no one else is able to help.

2. Breastfeeding can be uncomfortable. Most people find it uncomfortable at the beginning and eventually get used to it, but some moms just never like the sensation of breastfeeding and it does not get better for them.

3. It can be a little embarrassing at first. Babies do not always pick the most convenient times to want to eat and you are not always going to be in a room by yourself. Some women have a much harder time with this than others.

4. Breastfeeding can be very hard to do while working. Face it, most women have to work these days and it is hard to have the baby there at work with you. Depending on your job it can be hard to even find a place or time to pump breast milk to feed the baby.

5. It is all up to Mom. Someone else can feed breast milk to the baby through a bottle but all of it is has to come from Mom. With time this can get a little demanding and exhausting.

Whatever the pros or cons of breastfeeding versus bottle-feeding are, the real choice comes down to what Mom wants to do. All the pros in the world are not going to be worth it if Mom just does not want to breastfeed. There will be no bonding that occurs if you are doing something you hate. Babies will do fine breastfeeding or bottle feeding and you need to make sure that you surround yourself with people that will support and help you no matter what your decision is in this matter.

One of the common questions pediatricians get asked is what Mom can eat and drink while breastfeeding. A good rule of thumb is not to eat or drink anything you would not give a one year old. That rules out alcohol and drugs but everything else is fine. Individual babies may get bellyaches with certain foods but this will vary from baby to baby. Some of the most frequent offenders will be chocolate, caffeine, spicy foods, and broccoli, but everything is a possibility. If you find that your baby gets upset when you eat a certain food then you should try to avoid that food while you are breast-feeding.

So we have a newborn that is hungry and wants to eat. We need to feed him some milk in one form or another. If you have chosen to breastfeed, the first couple of days are going to be a little rough. The baby has no real idea how to eat and you have never done this before, so you have no idea how to help them. Almost all hospitals now have breastfeeding consultants that will be more than happy to help you get the hang of breastfeeding. They are great at teaching you methods to get your baby to latch on, for positioning them, and how to support Mom. The first couple days of breastfeeding you will just be producing colostrum. Colostrum is loaded with great antibodies, but is not very filling for your baby. If your baby starts to lose excessive amounts of weight, have blood sugar problems, or become jaundiced, your pediatrician may recommend that you give them some formula along with breast milk until you begin to produce more breast milk. Take your doctor's advice rather than the breastfeeding consultants; the pediatrician is trained to care for infants and to take responsibility for the baby's well being. After about 3-4 days your breast milk will kick in and your baby will not need any additional source of milk.

If you started out with formula you had an instant source of milk. The baby just needs to get the hang of a bottle, which they will figure out very quickly. When we first start feeding a baby they will typically take about half to one ounce every 2-3 hours. Over the first several days they will go up on the amount of milk they will drink. By the time they are a week old most babies will be taking two to three ounces every three hours. By the time they are a month old they will be taking four to six ounces every three to four hours. With the breastfeeding baby they typically take similar amounts of milk, you just do not have a way of measuring it. Newborn babies will usually breastfeed for 10-15 minutes per side. As the baby gets better at breast-feeding they will be able to take more milk in less time. By the time they are 2-3 weeks old it will only take them 7-15 minutes to eat (they may be there longer because they tend to fall asleep and just like to be warm and snuggly). The same is true for bottle fed babies. It will take quite a while to feed them just a little amount of formula, but after a couple of weeks they will be able to drain a bottle in just 5-10 minutes.

Let's talk about types of milk for your baby. As this book addresses babies from birth to two years of age we only need to discuss three types – breast milk, formula and whole milk.

Breast milk is fairly self-explanatory; it comes from Mom's breasts and there are not really different types. Just because it is nature's way to feed your baby does not necessarily mean that you will be able to breastfeed even if you want to. There are a few problems that may come up with breast-feeding. Some moms just do not produce any or enough milk. We are not sure why in most cases, but sometimes it is because Mom has had breast surgery such as augmentation or reductions, has unusual amounts of stress on her body or on some type of medication. Some moms produce enough fluid but it does not have enough calories for the baby to grow well. This will become evident when you see your pediatrician and have a baby that is eating well but is failing to grow normally. Finally, some babies just cannot tolerate breast milk because they are allergic to the protein in the milk. These problems will usually be found by or can be discussed with your pediatrician and they will let you know what, if any, options you have as far as improving breastfeeding or changing to a formula.

Formula is a little more complicated than breast milk because of the huge amount of varieties that you have to choose from. A baby should be started on a cow's milk based formula, because it will be the closest to human milk (a little piece of trivia: donkey's milk is the closest to humans, but harder to acquire). There are many types of cow's milk based formulas to choose from and every pediatrician or mom in the country probably has their preference. Let me just say that the formula industry is a big money earner and there is a lot of money spent on advertising by different formula companies to win business. Even your pediatrician's preference is probably going to be dictated by what a formula company has told them, how they have been treated by the company's representatives and of course their own personal experience. In an attempt to remain unbiased let me tell you that the companies are a lot like fast food. The ones that put the most money into advertising are the most expensive; they argue that they are also the ones that put the most money into research and quality control. This can be true but the difference in cost versus actual benefit may be questionable. My advice is that you ask your pediatrician what their recommendations are and why. Not all babies can tolerate cow's milk based formula and that is where the other types come in and the more expensive formulas you may see at the store. Switching to these other formulas should really be something that you should talk to your pediatrician about first before you make a switch. There are soy based formulas, formulas that have had the lactose removed, formulas with rice added to them, formulas that have had the proteins broken down so they can be used in babies allergic to milk protein, and formulas just made of amino acids. The specialty formulas are much more expensive and are not best for your baby if they do not need them.

Formula or breast milk should be the only type of milk your baby is given for the first year of life. Yes, whole milk is in the refrigerator already and is cheaper, but it does not have the vitamins, minerals, iron or type of protein a baby's body needs to grow properly. At one year of age it is fine to switch your baby to whole milk. Because whole milk is not a complete food source, a baby only needs about 12-20 ounces of milk a day. A baby does need to use whole milk until two years of age because it needs the fat for its brain to grow properly. At two years of age you can switch to two percent milk.

Many books will tell you exactly how much milk your baby should drink or how long they should breastfeed each time. There is no "exact" amount of milk that a baby should drink; each baby's needs are different. As long as your baby is growing and developing well, the amount they eat is fine. The numbers that are printed in books are just guidelines so you have an idea of how much a baby should eat. Here are some guidelines to give you an idea of the eating estimations for each age.

1-2 days	½-1 ounce ever 2-3 hours
3-5 days	1-2 ½ ounces every 3-4 hours
6-30 days	Increasing to 4-6 ounces every 3-4 hours
1-2 months	6-8 ounces on demand which is usually every 3-4 hours
2-6 months	6 plus ounces (this is typically the most milk they will drink in their lives) as desired. These babies are able to go up to 12 hours without eating.
6-12 months	as much as they want to eat each time but realize that they will drink less each time because they are now getting food as well. Most babies will get 20-36 ounces per day.
12-24 months	these babies will now be on whole milk and need 12-20 ounces per day. Whole milk is not a complete food source like breast milk or formula and needs to be limited.

For the first four months of life your baby should not get anything to eat or drink except formula or breast milk. There are special conditions in which your doctor may add something else, but they should not have anything else unless directed to do so by your doctor. A baby does not need any water except what is given in their milk because too much water can lower their body salts and can lead to health problems. A baby does not need any juice and should not be given any until they are six months of age. No matter what people tell you, feeding your new baby cereal or baby food will not get them to sleep through the night and can lead to health problems. Babies that have an early introduction of cereals and foods to their diet have been found to have worse allergies, eczema, asthma and constipation. We have learned many things about parenting since your parents raised you so listen to your pediatrician.

When the baby is four to six months old it is time to introduce them to solid foods. There are several ways to introduce solids to your baby and I am merely going to explain my way. Most pediatricians follow these guidelines closely with just the odd variation here and there, which is usually dependent on the way we were trained. A baby is developmentally able to start baby foods between the ages of four and six months. All babies do not arrive at this time simultaneously. I have found that a good way of telling if a baby is ready to eat solids is if they watch you intensely while you are eating and are opening their mouth like they want to eat some. If you start trying to feed your baby with a spoon and they just sputter and gag on the food they are not ready yet. Wait a week or so and then try it again. Just keep trying until they suddenly become able to swallow without gagging and choking, but you do not have to try it everyday. I personally recommend trying once a week to see if they are ready.

Babies with a family history of eczema, food allergies or asthma or who have had wheezing or eczema themselves should wait until they are six months to start on solid foods. There have been several studies that show by waiting until six months the incidence of these conditions decreases. The American Academy of Pediatrics, the World Health Organization and most breastfeeding authorities recommend waiting until six months.

We all recommend you only feed your baby solids with a spoon. There are many things you will find at the stores to feed your baby solids with but these are not recommended by pediatricians and can cause serious problems. Do not add food to the bottle, do not use syringe-feeding systems and do not use little bag contraptions that let them suck on the food and "filter" it through. If your baby cannot eat with a spoon they are not ready to eat solid food yet.

I recommend that parents start off with rice cereal mixed with either expressed breast milk or formula as a training food until the baby gets good at eating with a spoon. It will vary from baby to baby how long it takes them to master the act of swallowing but once they get good at swallowing the cereal, it is time to start them on baby foods and never eat rice cereal again.

Baby foods are categorized as stage I, stage II, stage III, graduates, and finger foods. That is also the order that we will progress through them with a little blurb describing each type of baby food. Stage I foods are the little jars that tend to be the most runny of the baby foods and are all single entity in content. Stage II is a slightly bigger jar, has a thicker consistency, and starts to mix food types together. Stage III is an even bigger jar, has food with little pieces and chunks and again mixes types of foods together. Graduates are mainly there as table foods substitute if you do not want to take the time to cut up your food in small enough pieces or are eating something not for babies. Finger foods are going to be the things that babies start to feed themselves with their fingers like teether biscuits, veggie puffs, vanilla wafers, and crackers.

Babies prefer sugar in the beginning, so I like to introduce foods in the order of least sugar to most. This is an area that we as doctors often disagree on without any real medical studies to back any of us up. I have just found that if a baby has had fruits first it is very hard to get them to eat less sugar containing foods like green beans afterwards. Therefore I recommend starting with green vegetables, then orange and yellow vegetables and finally fruits. Because we are introducing new foods into their diet, we may find the baby develops an allergy to one of these new foods. Therefore I recommend that you only introduce a new food every 3-5 days. With this schedule you would do green beans for 3-5 days, then peas for 3-5 days and so on. Food allergies will usually present as hives (which are red swollen splotches on your baby's body) or as patches of dry, red skin called eczema. It will take about a month and a half to get through all the single entities and then you can mix and match the types of food. Once a baby goes through all the types and acts like the small jars are not enough food, it is time to go up to the next stage. This is my way and there are as many different ways out there as there are pediatricians; the funny thing is they all are right in their own way.

Every baby is different and you should not compare how much your baby eats with what other babies are eating. They should eat enough for them. As they eat more and more solid food, they will drink less milk. We usually want a baby eating three times a day by the time they are nine months old, but the amount they eat could vary from three stage I jars per day to nine stage III jars per day.

When babies are between six and nine months and able to sit up on their own and eat their baby foods, then it is time to introduce some finger foods. We usually start out with bulky, finger foods that dissolve in their mouths. These are foods like teether biscuits, zwieback toast, and vanilla wafers. Once a baby gets good at these foods, then it is time to move to things that can be bitten like crackers and then on to small things like goldfish and cheerios. In this period it is fine to start introducing some table foods that are the consistency of baby food.

After six months of age babies can start drinking some juice or water. We do not want them to get more than about six ounces per day. It is also important to note they do not "need" any as the fluid they need is given through their milk, but the juice and water are a great way to introduce a baby to a sippy cup and rewarding them for learning a new skill.

I usually want my babies to be eating table food by the time they are one year old. Many parents will want to give them the little graduate meals because they are easier to prepare and are convenient and these are fine as well. The amount a baby will eat will vary from baby to baby. Make sure they are getting a variety of meats, vegetables and fruits, dairy and grains.

A baby will grow at a consistent rate for the first 12-15 months and their appetite will be fairly predictable. Around the time they are 15-18 months of age they start growing in spurts. During this time the amount they are grow per year slows way down and there will be times they do not seem to eat much at all. This is when all parents freak out and think their baby is going to starve to death. The baby will be fine; I have not lost one yet to voluntarily not eating. Just keep offering them a good variety of foods and they will eat when they need to. This period is probably our healthiest because we eat based on our metabolic rate. The worst thing we probably teach our children is to eat three meals whether they are hungry or not.

THINGS TO REMEMBER:

-Only formula or breast milk for the first 4-6 months

-Only formula or breast milk as a milk source for the first year

-Whole milk from one to two years old

-I introduce food as green veggies then orange and yellow vegetables, then fruits

-NO HONEY FOR THE FIRST YEAR

-Only give solid food with a spoon

-No table food until they are six to nine months old

-Never taste baby food, it is disgusting!

-If your parents and grandparents really did the stuff they say you would have died.

Kaden's logs

December 17, 2011

Today was a monumental day in my life. There are so few days in a person's life that they can say are truly life changing, but today was one of them for me. Today was the day I got to eat something besides MOO. I had this day in my head since I first noticed that other people got to eat something other than MOO. I had my first menu all laid out in my head. I was going to have a nice 9 oz. fillet steak cooked medium rare, a large rock lobster tail steamed to perfection and drizzled with garlic butter, and a baked potato stuffed with sour cream, butter, cheese and bacon. I was even going to eat a green vegetable just to be a good example for the little people. I was going to top it off with a seven layer chocolate cake and wash it down with a large glass of ice cold Mountain Dew. Unfortunately I have not yet learned to talk. (I'm thinking that will be another life changing moment). Instead of my menu my parents fed me what can only be described as gruel. It was white, watery, fairly gross, tasteless cereal made of rice. Do I look Chinese? I don't want rice. I am a red-blooded American male. I want to go from drinking MOO to eating the producer of MOO. I AM A CARNIVORE! But no, my parents have reduced me to eating gruel. I'm sure it is no different than what they fed prisoners in medieval times. Don't fret or worry about me, I am going to take up arms and find me some real food. I will become the Robin Hood of my day. I will work to steal the food from the people who have it and give to the people who don't (which from my point of view seems to be me).

December 29, 2011

My daddy is some kind of sick, twisted individual. I have been suffering through the poisonous green beans for the last four days. Today I made it through the torture knowing that soon I would get to try something new. Daddy said he liked peas much better than green beans. I had my suspicions based on Mommy and Bubby's reaction to the word peas, but I trusted my daddy. Today arrived and Daddy fed me my peas. Or what I should say is he shoved a gross concoction of vile green slime down my throat. My mommy was so right, peas SUCK! Guess what? My daddy is going to make me eat this rot for the next two days. I will be thinking bad thoughts about him while he sleeps. I don't see him trying this disgusting slime. Mommy at least tries it and tries to hide her nasty face. Daddy just smiles at me and just keeps shoving it in. I have got to learn how to distract him and get rid of it somehow. I would feed it to our dog except I'm afraid it would kill him. I hope I live through the next two days.

CHAPTER 5

Things that make you go YUCK!
(Pee, poop, puke and snot)

A very cute baby, but everything that exits them is disgusting.

This chapter is dedicated to the four things making up at least 70 percent of the phone calls coming into a pediatrician's office. Who knows, this book may be responsible for reducing a pediatrician staff's workload. These four things generate the most questions and most will be answered and explained here. Trust me when I say this is the one chapter you read that will save you some serious worrying and money.

We will start off with number one, which is fitting isn't it? Trust me when I say you will be around urine, the golden stuff of dreams, so much that you will probably have some dreams about it too. Urine is the waste-water of the body. Your kidneys filter your blood and remove any excess fluid, salts and toxins and it exits the body as urine. The amount of urine you produce will be determined by the amount of fluid you take in. The color of urine is determined by what is being removed from the body and the smell is determined by what is coming out as well.

There are some important points to make about urine. A baby should have at least four wet diapers per day. If they do not have four wet diapers, we start to worry they may not be getting enough fluids and may become dehydrated. We get a bunch of questions concerning the amount of wet diapers and the possibility of diabetes. Diabetes is very rare in babies and will not just present with lots of diapers (they will also be losing weight and getting very sick). Many people worry about different types of smells or color in the urine and think the baby has a urinary tract infection. Most babies with urinary tract infections have normal looking and smelling urine. A baby with a urinary tract infection may present with a fever, vomiting or is just very fussy. You will need to call your pediatrician if their urine is extremely foul smelling, red in color or they cry when voiding. If a baby boy has a urine stream that is just a dribble or shoots off to the side, you should ask your pediatrician about this on your next well visit. It is very normal for a little boy to get an erection when they need to urinate so do not worry about this.

Moving on to number two, or poop, we come to the number one reason a pediatrician gets called. People are very concerned about their baby's poop. Hopefully this discussion will be helpful to you and not make you feel ill. Poop or stool is formed by what your body did not want to absorb from what you ate and drank. The smell, color, and texture of stool are determined by what your body needs and what you eat.

A newborn passes meconium for the first couple of days. This is a thick, tar-black stool made up of sloughed skin cells while a baby is developing. It forms a plug to keep a baby from stooling before they are born. When a baby is born, they will start passing the meconium until the plug is gone. (Do note that meconium is just like trying to get tar off their little bottoms; it is gross, but at least it does not smell).

Once a baby is done with the meconium they will start passing what we call normal baby poop. Normal baby poop is usually yellowish-green and the consistency of watery cottage cheese. (Note that I use cottage cheese to describe it because I think cottage cheese is gross). Breastfed babies tend to have more watery stools that are more yellowish in color. Formula fed baby's stools are a little thicker and may have more of a green color. Babies have a reflex making their colon contract whenever their stomach fills. This will mean for the first two to four weeks a baby could have a dirty diaper after every feeding. This means you will be changing tons of dirty diapers. Between three and five weeks of age this reflex will go away and a baby will start to slow down on pooping. This is when pediatricians will get calls from parents thinking their baby is constipated. When the reflex to stool goes a baby will not know how to poop and will push every muscle in their little body, strain, turn bright red and scream like they are mad or in pain. I am sure the people making gas relievers make most of their money during this stage of life. Despite the baby's efforts to push, the only thing that comes out sometimes is gas. Because they have a fussy baby who is passing gas, parents assume their baby is having gas pain. In actuality, the baby is just mad because it cannot figure out how to poop and is straining and passing gas. It will take about two weeks for the baby to figure out which muscles to push and figure out how to get the poop out.

After this stage a baby will vary how often they pass stool, but it will be much less than it was the first month. Some babies tend to go several days without passing stool and other babies will have several stools per day. The consistency will vary from baby to baby and can be anywhere from watery cottage cheese (I just hate that stuff) to peanut butter (I like this but I couldn't think of another descriptor). The stool should never come out as hard balls. This is constipation and it will hurt to pass. Be sure to call your pediatrician about constipation. It is better to ask what they recommend than to take the many different recommendations you will get from your friends and family.

Stool color may vary depending on what your baby is eating and what they need to absorb. As pediatricians, we really only care about three colors of stool: red, black and white. Red and black are indicative of blood and white means fat is not being absorbed properly. All the other colors are acceptable. If red, black and white present they should always be discussed with your pediatrician.

Speaking of green and nasty, we might as well talk about snot. Bet you never dreamed of becoming an adult so you could chase a little toddler around trying to pick a nasty booger out of their nose...welcome to your new life. Your baby will not only have stuff come out of its nose but chances are a few things will go up its nose as well. Mucous is produced to moisten the inside of the nose and as a way to humidify the air before it goes into the lungs. An adult produces about one liter of mucous a day, a baby a little less. Depending on the thickness of the mucous it will have different colors. When it runs fast it is clear, as it gets thicker it will be yellow and when it is very thick it will be kind of green. You should not see thick white mucous (this could be pus, but is most likely milk coming out their nose). You should not have foul smelling mucous (this is infection and is usually indicative something has gotten stuck up in the nose (things like tissue, beads, food and the like). Blood tinged mucous will be common if your baby has had its nose wiped or sucked out frequently.

There are several things that may cause more snot to come out of your baby's nose. After six months of age a baby can start to develop allergies to things they are around constantly like dust mites, cats, and mold. Babies will tend to get between seven and 10 colds per year, more if they go to daycare or have older siblings in school. Babies' noses can run when they are teething, which can happen anytime between two and 18 months. Anything making a baby's eyes water will make their nose run, because tear ducts drain tears into their noses.

There are not many things you can do for a baby's snotty nose. If their nose is plugged up you can suction it out with a bulb suction syringe. Sucking out a baby's nose is made easer if you put a few drops of normal saline into the nostril before sucking it out. Normal saline nose drops can be found under many different brands at your local pharmacy and are a good thing to have around if you have a baby. Babies do not like when their nose is plugged up, so they actually do better if their nose is running. A vaporizer or humidifier to increase the humidity in the air will help a baby by making its mucous thinner. If your baby suffers from allergies your pediatrician may recommend some medicine to help their symptoms, but you should only give them if your doctor recommends them. There are no medicines currently recommended for babies less than two to help with their runny noses from colds.

They will pick their nose, they will eat their boogers, and they will suck snot back into their throat and swallow it. They will also lick the snot off their upper lip when it is running. It is gross. It is disgusting. It will not hurt them one bit. Remember when I told you an adult produces one liter of mucous a day? Did you blow your nose today? If so did you get a liter out? No, because it runs down the back of your throat and you swallow it all day long and it does not hurt you one bit. Work on their manners over time but do not freak out in the short run.

Of all the things on the "yuck" list, the worst one, in my opinion, is vomit. I can handle a little spit up with a burp, but vomiting in front of me just makes me want to hurl too. Trust me when I say your child will cure you of this problem. One night my little guy decided to get sick and vomit all night long. The first time he baptized himself and his bed. The second time he baptized himself, my bed and me. Before I could get the mess cleaned up he had baptized us both again. I put some sheets on the couch and thought I would just sleep there, but he got us both again as well as the sheets. I finally gave up and we just slept in the bathtub so I could just rinse us off each time he threw up…all 11 times. I have now successfully been cured of my reflexive vomiting.

Your baby will spit up. They all spit up in varying degrees. Chances are they will at sometime have a vomiting and diarrhea illness. I will try to discuss the differences and what to do for each.

Most of a baby's spit-ups are just that, spitting up some stuff. This can happen if they get choked by sucking spit or milk down the wrong tube or by having some come up when they burp. Wet burps happen when a baby has gas in their stomach that needs to come up and it brings some milk along with it as it comes up. These wet burps are the most common when babies are very small in the first six months of life. Babies tend to burp less as they get older and therefore have less wet burps. These spit-ups can be minimized by frequent burping, avoiding over feeding and making sure a baby is not lying flat right after eating.

Gastroesophageal reflux is when stomach contents such as food or milk come up from the stomach and into the esophagus and sometimes right out the mouth. Wet burps are a mild form of reflux and therefore all babies will have some reflux. In some babies this is much worse than just a little spit up now and then. If your baby is spitting up copious amounts of milk with every feeding, you should discuss this with your pediatrician. Depending upon the extent of the reflux or if any problems are arising such as poor weight gain or apnea, your doctor may recommend medicines, further work-up by a GI specialist (stomach doctor), or some simple things to minimize spit-ups. Do not take matters into your own hands and start following advice from friends or family or switching formulas.

Vomiting with illness is something every baby will probably face at some time or another. Vomiting in a baby is probably a good reason to give your doctor a call if it happens more than twice. If your baby has thrown up more than twice in a short time then you know you have vomiting and not just spit up. There are many reasons a baby might vomit and some of these can be very serious. The list includes, but is not limited to, a virus, strep throat, urinary tract infections, serious bacterial illnesses, and meningitis. It is not your job to figure out why they are vomiting – this is why you have pediatricians so use them.

Treating vomiting will of course vary depending on the cause of the vomiting, but I can give you some clues of things to look for which can make your pediatrician's job easier. You need to pay attention to how often you are changing your baby's wet diapers. Also keep track of dirty diapers and how watery they are. Take your baby's temperature. If your baby throws up, wait awhile before giving them something to drink again. Usually waiting at least an hour before giving them something to drink is a good idea, since it will give their stomach a chance to settle. Find out if your little one has been exposed to any illnesses or had any new foods. These little pieces of information will make it a lot easier for your baby's doctor to figure out what is going on with your baby.

Kaden's logs

September 22, 2011

I have gotten used to peeing and pooping on myself. I had that episode of vomiting that kind of shocked me and I have spit on myself from time to time. Today I added a new secretion to my repertoire when I found I could make a slimy substance run out of my nose. It has some possibilities so I think there may be pros and cons. I have learned from my parents that this substance is called snot. I have found my snot to be stretchy when I get some on my fingers. When I smear it on my face it dries and turns a pretty yellow. I think it will be fun to share with other people. I'm not sure but it may be a form of food...at least I saw a little kid eat some earlier today.

It does seem to have some cons. It is hard to eat when you can't breathe through your nose. It also makes me sound funny when I take a breath and it makes me cough. My voice sounds funny and it seems to worry my mommy. Daddy seems less worried...I'm going to pee on him later.

My snot seems to also be a cause for discussion at my house. My mommy thinks Daddy brought me home a cold. Daddy has tried to blame my brothers and their school, my pediatrician and the office, and he secretly thinks the sore throat my mommy is complaining about is the source of my snot. I'm just trying to figure out how this slimy substance is going to help me conquer the world. If you have any uses for this snot please let me know.

January 13, 2012

I have added a new illness to my list today. They say that Friday the 13th brings bad luck and some certainly descended upon me today. Today I got to learn about the joys of diarrhea. I went shopping at the mall with my mommy today. I must admit I wasn't feeling myself all day and had been kind of a grump. I had even cried when my daddy came home for lunch, which is normally my "happy" time. Anyway Mommy and I were shopping when all of a sudden a foul smelling explosion like a backfire happened in my pants. My mommy could tell right away by the smell that a diaper change was in order. She took me to the restroom to change my pants only to discover that my poop runneth over. When I say runneth over I mean it had came out of me like a runaway lava flow. I had poop in the diaper, I had poop up my back, all over my clothes, into my socks and down to my toes. When Mommy tried to change me she even got a fair share of my poop on her. Upon further investigation she found I had even managed to poop on my car seat. An extensive changing procedure occurred and I exited the restroom wearing a brand new outfit with most of me scrubbed clean.

We met Daddy for supper and while my parents were eating I made my poopy face and once again an evil smell exited my body. Mommy said it was Daddy's turn to change the poopy diaper. She handed Daddy a diaper, wipes and a changing pad and we were off to the restroom. All was going well when my Daddy discovered my potential as a human volcano as not only was my diaper disgusting, but so were my onsie and my jumpsuit. Daddy was in a quandary; he had me in a new diaper but my clothes were covered in poop and his cell phone was at the table with Mommy. Guess who got to be paraded around the restaurant mostly naked wearing only a diaper? Yep, my daddy was once again responsible for ruining my future social life. I got taken out to the table to get some new clothes and then we went back to the restroom again. My only saving grace was the outfit I came out wearing was so different to the one I wore into the restaurant and my mostly naked body, that no one probably recognized me. It was funny to watch Daddy's face turn red while everyone looked at him hauling a half naked baby around. I don't feel so great and my belly is sure making some nasty noises, but this is the first illness I've had that was somewhat funny. It is something evidently my family wants to share as Mommy is now sick and Daddy isn't looking so good himself. We may stay mostly in this weekend.

CHAPTER 6

Shoot 'em up
(vaccines)

I dedicate this cartoon to John Kittle...
because we all long for this shot.

Vaccines are one of the things that are harder on parents than babies. It is hard for us as parents who are supposed to protect our babies from harm to willingly allow them to feel pain. It is in the feeling of reluctance to hurt our babies that the anti-vaccine movement finds its audience. When we do not want to do something we look for something to support our opinions. Unfortunately, there have been some famous personalities who have stepped up and filled that role and have made it harder and harder for doctors to persuade people to vaccinate their children. My goal is not to necessarily persuade you to vaccinate your child (which is a very good idea), but provide you with the background details about why we vaccinate and how vaccines work.

The first thing you need to understand about vaccines is a term called immunity. Immunity in simple terms is a body's ability to remember something it has had before and keeps from getting it again. A disease attacks the body either as a bacteria, virus, or yeast. The body needs to respond to fight off the infection to keep from dying. The body has cells responsible for recognizing anything foreign or dangerous that enters it. Through a series of steps, the body starts to produce antibodies to fight off the illness to remove it from the body. Their cells store the memory of how to make these antibodies. If the body is ever attacked again by the same disease it can immediately start production of the antibodies to keep the disease from causing illness.

Some diseases are so severe they can lead to severe illness, disability or even death before the body has time to produce antibodies to fight off the illness. Before the production of vaccines, disease such as smallpox, polio, tetanus, whooping cough, strep pneumonia, hemophilus influenza, diphtheria, measles and mumps often led to disability and death. It was the severity of the illnesses that stimulated so much research and money being spent on the development of vaccines to prevent them.

The idea of a vaccine is to stimulate the body to produce antibodies to fight off an illness and to keep the memory without the person ever getting the disease. Vaccines have been designed using the actual virus that has been weakened with pieces of the virus or bacteria, by using other bacteria incapable of causing disease in humans, or a milder illness still able to produce immunity. Once a substitute is discovered scientists have to find a safe way to "infect" the person with the vaccine so the vaccine produces immunity to the real illness, but does not harm the person.

Vaccines have worked so well over the last 40 years parents have become more scared of the vaccines than they are of the disease. The main reason for this is because diseases are seen so rarely many people believe they are gone. Unfortunately the diseases still exist and if given the chance and a population of people with no immunity, they will thrive and cause disease, disability and death again.

Before we give all the credit of a disease free planet to the vaccines it should be mentioned that good sanitation, pest control, safe food and water supplies and medical care such as hospitals and medication have done an equal share of prevention and treatment for many of these illnesses. Many of the anti-vaccine people would like to give these advances all the credit for decreasing these diseases and many of the pro-vaccine group would like to downplay their importance.

Here is where I get to put my two cents into the discussion. When it comes to my children and my patients I want to prevent them from getting sick with any disease leading to their disability or death. With that in mind I want to use everything available to me. I recommend healthy living, good diet, safe homes, and vaccines that have been well tested and proven effective and safe. If those things fail then we use medical treatments to treat the illness. Would you want to go to a mechanic to fix your car who refused to use any tool except a hammer, or go to a school only teaching subtraction in math, or a doctor who treated people only by changing their diet? I know when I want something done I want them to use every tool at their disposal to get the job done right.

There have been other people who do not like the idea of giving multiple vaccines at the same time and want to alter the vaccination schedule. In that regard, I would have to defer to your doctor. There are certain vaccines, for which the schedule can be changed some, but in others there is a set timeline to give them and certain vaccines that either have to be given at the same time or separated by a given time. Many people just want to base this decision on pain they feel their child will feel from multiple vaccines. My response to these parents would be to ask them if they would prefer to have one bad day or multiple bad days? Would you rather drop a brick and smash all your toes at once and feel all the pain, or smash your big toe today, the second in a week, the third a couple days later, the fourth on another day and the fifth a couple of days later? I want to get it over all at once, because it is all just pain and I would rather have one day of pain than multiple days of pain.

Some people say vaccines cause autism. These arguments change, as they are proven wrong. The original argument was the MMR vaccine caused autism. When MMR was shown to not cause autism, then the thimerosal preservative was blamed. When thimerosal was removed from the vaccines, then it was the amount of vaccines given to shoulder the blame. The scientific community has proven each of the theories false, but the other side just changes how they blame vaccines without having to prove anything on their side of the argument.

Parents often don't know what the actual disease does that we are seeking to prevent. Why do we want to prevent it from happening? How do babies get it from people? What would happen if we stopped vaccinating everyone? In the section below I describe what the diseases we vaccinate against in these first two years are and why we need to vaccinate against them.

Hepatitis B: Hepatitis B is a virus transmitted by exchange of blood products, like blood transfusions and sharing needles or by unprotected sex. It can also be transmitted from an infected mother to her baby. Moms sometimes do not even have symptoms of the disease, since it can take up to six months from the infection to develop symptoms. Babies are much more likely to develop chronic liver disease which leads to liver failure and the need for liver transplants than adults are when contracting Hepatitis B. Many people argue babies do not need this vaccine because they will not be doing drugs or having sex until they are older. Unfortunately we do not get to plan when they may need a blood transfusion and we never know when they might step on an infected needle or get poked with one in a trash can as they walk by. Hepatitis is an extinguishable disease and once everyone is immunized it will go away just like smallpox has done in the recent past.

Diphtheria: Diphtheria is a disease caused by the bacteria *Corynebacterium diphtheriae*. Do not worry there will not be a test on how to say or spell that little booger. It is a bacteria spread through the air when people cough or sneeze, but can also be transmitted through contaminated food or by putting something in their mouth that has been contaminated with the bacteria. It mainly affects the nose and throat and causes a gray to black membrane to form. Unfortunately it does not just stop with a really sore throat, but can lead to heart damage and damage to your nervous system which may cause paralysis. If infected it has a 10 percent mortality rate and if you do not die recovery is very slow. We do not hear about this disease much in the US because of our widespread immunization but it still exists in other countries. In 1994 there were about 50,000 cases in Russia. Foreign people who may have been infected before coming to the United States are still exposing us.

Tetanus: Tetanus is the cause of the infection known as lockjaw and is caused by the bacteria, *Clostridium tetani*. This bacteria lives inactive as a spore in the ground and may be infectious for up to 40 years. It gets into the body through a wound contaminated by dirt. It leads to muscle spasms called tetani that resemble seizures. It can cause these spasms in your jaw, which does not allow you to open your mouth, but can also happen to any of the muscle groups in the body including your airway. If untreated, one in three people will die. Properly treated the death rate in children is less than 10 percent. Because of vaccinations in the United States we only see five cases per year and these are in unimmunized people or people who have not had their boosters. There are approximately one million cases per year worldwide.

Pertussis: A disease otherwise known as whooping cough caused by *Bordetella pertussis* or *Bordetella parapertussis*. It is a bacterial infection starting with a fever and cough that continues to get worse. After the first two weeks the cough gets deeper and the patient begins to cough up an abundance of mucous that may lead to vomiting. They may cough in such prolonged fits their breathing is affected and they may not get enough oxygen to their brain. It is especially deadly in small infants. Pertussis can lead to choking, seizures, mental retardation, apnea (when breathing stops for periods greater than 20 seconds), and death. With our immunizations in the United States we usually only see outbreaks in infants (before they can get the vaccine), unimmunized patients, or in older people who have not had a booster of pertussis vaccine.

Hemophilus type B: This vaccine is aptly named for *Hemophilus influenza* type B bacteria – it's amazing that for once in medicine the names make sense. This is a nasty little bacteria and before the vaccine came out it was the leading cause of bacterial meningitis in children less than five years of age and the second leading bacterial cause of pneumonia and ear infections. The most severe infection was of course the development of meningitis that, even when treated, had a 3-5 percent incidence of death, a 20 percent incidence of hearing loss in the survivors and could cause seizures and mental retardation. Today with proper vaccines it is a very uncommon infection in children once they have been adequately vaccinated. It is still a very real threat to young infants who have not started their vaccines.

Polio: Polio has been fairly effectively wiped off the planet by a worldwide vaccination program. Polio has been rare in the United States since the early 1970s. In 2000 we converted to using a shot instead of an oral polio vaccine, because the oral polio vaccine was a live vaccine and was the only cause of polio we were continuing to see in the United States. The vaccine we use now is called IPV, or inactivated polio vaccine, and is incapable of causing disease. In 2013 the world was down to 416 cases of polio. Once polio has been eradicated then vaccination for it will no longer be needed.

Streptococcus pneumonia: Prevnar is the current vaccine for *Streptococcal pneumonia* and is one of the newer vaccines given to our babies. It has been routinely given for the last 15 years and has been a Godsend to babies. *Streptococcus pneumonia* is a bacterial infection, which, following the intro-duction of HIB vaccine was the leading cause of bacterial meningitis and is the leading cause of bacterial pneumonia and ear infections in children. This bacteria is nothing like its cousin the bacteria that causes strep throat and is truly a bacteria to be feared. Symptoms from strep pneumonia are going to vary depending on where the infection is located. It can cause a secondary infection such as pneumonia, ear or sinus infections and symp-toms related to those conditions. It can cause meningitis with symptoms of stiff neck, vomiting, and high fever so you look like death warmed up. It can also cause a condition called bacteremia where the bacteria are in your blood. Your only symptom for this will be extremely high fever and chills. The treatments always include antibiotics, but in the cases of meningitis, bacteremia and pneumonia you can end up in hospital for treatment. Unfortunately sometimes treatment is not enough and babies die from these infections. The vaccine has done a lot to reduce these diseases in the last 10-15 years. This is not one of the vaccines you would ever want to skip.

Rotavirus: Rotavirus is a virus that does exactly what it sounds like. It acts like a rotating rooter on your intestinal tract and leaves no blockage or any-thing else in there (boy, I would like to use a nationally known sewer clean-ing company name in that sentence). This is the largest killer of children worldwide, mainly in third world countries. Most deaths are secondary to severe dehydration. Rotavirus causes a severe, watery diarrhea, which just seems to shoot out like a very foul-smelling, green, poopy fountain. The diarrhea can be severe with 15-30 stools a day not uncommon. This is never good for a little one and unfortunately often requires I.V. fluids and hospi-talization. Rotavirus has a new vaccine that started being used widely in the mid-2000s and has several new vaccines in the pipeline. This vaccine has been worth its weight in solid gold poop. I went from putting in about 75 IVs a year during rotavirus season to none last year.

Varicella: Otherwise known as the chickenpox. The virus Varicella-zoster, a member of the herpes family, causes it. It started being widely vaccinated against in the late 1990s and has decreased the incidence of chickenpox immensely. Parents often question whether we need to vaccinate against chickenpox since it is a benign viral illness. Chickenpox used to be very common, but was responsible for over 100 deaths per year in the United States and every child with chickenpox missed about 10-14 days of school. With our need these days for a two income family how many people can afford to take off two weeks to stay at home with their child? How many children can keep up in school if they miss two weeks? I do not know how you feel, but to me if any child dies from a mild illness it is unacceptable if it can be prevented.

Hepatitis A: Hepatitis A virus causes hepatitis, as you might suspect. Hepatitis is a swelling and inflammation of the liver. It is spread through contaminated stools from infected individuals and is transmitted through contaminated food or water. This is a fairly new vaccine that is now recommended to everyone, having been previously only recommended to people in high-risk areas, such as flood plains. With recent outbreaks of hepatitis from restaurants thanks to contaminated vegetables, the Center for Disease Control recommended it be a universal recommended vaccine to try to eliminate it from the population. Many find its use controversial because it is a self-limited disease, meaning is usually resolves on its own, and very rarely fatal. The great thing is it has few, if any vaccine reactions.

Measles/Mumps/Rubella: A combination shot otherwise known as the MMR. I will try to tell you what the diseases are and what they did and leave the controversy about their vaccine to your doctor to talk to you about, since this will probably change over time depending on which celebrities are currently on talk shows acting like doctors.

<u>**Measles:**</u> The classical symptoms of measles include four days of fevers, coughing, runny noses and conjunctivitis. The fever may reach up to 104 degrees F. The characteristic measles rash is classically described as a red, bumpy rash beginning several days after the first symptoms and may last eight days. Complications of the measles are relatively common, ranging from the relatively mild and less serious like diarrhea and dehydration, to conjunctivitis, which can lead to corneal ulcers as well as infections of the lung and brain. Complications are usually more severe amongst adults who catch the virus.

Mumps: The most common symptom is inflammation of the parotid (a salivary gland along the jaw line) in about 60-70 percent of infections and 95 percent of patients with symptoms. Parotitis causes swelling and local pain, particularly when chewing. It can occur on one side, but is more common on both sides. Fevers can be as high as 101-104 degrees Fahrenheit. Orchitis is a painful inflammation of the testicle. Males who are past puberty have about a 30 percent chance of developing orchitis. Following orchitis the testicles can atrophy (get smaller) and can rarely cause sterility (orchitis alone is enough for me to wholeheartedly recommend the mumps vaccine). Mumps can also cause severe headache (if you could notice it amongst the other terrible symptoms). Mumps is a contagious disease spread from person to person through contact with respiratory secretions such as saliva from an infected person. When an infected person coughs or sneezes, the droplets aerosolize and can enter the eyes, nose or mouth of another person. Sharing food and drinks can also spread mumps. The virus can also survive on surfaces and then be spread after contact in a similar manner. A person infected with mumps is contagious from approximately six days before the onset of symptoms until about nine days after symptoms start. Death is very unusual. The disease is usually self-limiting and the general outcome is good, even if other organs are involved.

Rubella: Rubella is commonly known as the German three-day measles. It is a very mild infection; usually not causing many problems unless contracted while the person is pregnant. If contracted during the first trimester of pregnancy it can lead to spontaneous abortion about 27 percent of the time. It causes symptoms similar to the flu. The first symptom is a rash on the face spreading to the body and usually fades after about three days. It can also cause low-grade fever, swollen lymph nodes, joint pains, headache and pink eye. Fever is rarely over 100.4 degrees F.

The main reason a vaccine is given is to prevent congenital rubella syndrome. This happens if a mother acquires rubella during the first trimester. If the baby survives the infection they can go on to develop cardiac, brain, eye and hearing defects. It can also lead to prematurity, low birth weight, anemia, and hepatitis. The baby can also be born with a severe rash called blueberry muffin baby syndrome.

Many of these diseases you have probably never even heard about, much less even seen. Their rareness is a true testimony of how well vaccines work. In countries not giving these vaccines, some of the diseases are alive and well and kill babies every day. As a medical community we are striving to continue to develop new vaccines to further prevent disease. There are currently vaccines for strep throat, Alzheimer's disease, HIV, genital herpes and malaria being developed. It is far better to prevent an illness from ever happening than try to treat it after you get the disease.

Think about all the things you do to protect your baby. You put outlet covers all over your house, block all the stairways, lock up medications and always put your child in their car seat. In 2011 650 children less than 14 years of age died in car accidents. In the same year 158,000 people died from measles worldwide. There are reasons vaccines are given and exist even if you do not know or remember why.

There will always be people that take an opposing stance. There are people who refuse to take any medicines, accept blood transfusions, and eat non-organic foods. They have every right to their opinions and choices. The important things to do as a parent is understand the facts. When someone gives you advice about how to care for your child, ask yourself if you would trust the person to take care of your child.

Chapter 7

Happy birthday

There are many things you should remember to bring to the hospital…just don't forget the mom!

Y ou have now made it to the hospital for the baby's big arrival. Well hopefully you have made it to the hospital; I have had several babies born at home, in the car or in the parking lot of the hospital. Things have probably already not gone according to plan. Dad may have forgotten half the stuff he was supposed to remember yet still managed to bring a moving van's worth of stuff and everyone is a nervous wreck.

We should start with some basics. What do you absolutely need for the baby while you are in the hospital? Luckily if you have forgotten everything you will be fine. The hospital has assumed you are idiots and will have everything you will need while you are there. It is a good idea to have some clothes to bring the baby home in and to take the all important hospital picture. You will need a car seat you have properly installed or the hospital will not let you put the baby into the car to take it home. (Most fire departments and some police stations will check to make sure your seat is properly installed and it is a good idea to let them help you before the baby arrives, as they require almost rocket science to install). You will also need some receiving blankets to wrap the baby up to take it home. The hospital will have gowns, diapers, ointment, milk and everything you could possibly need while you are there.

So the time for the baby to get here has arrived. You have heard all your friends and family say how pretty their babies were when they were born. Your baby arrives, they hold it up for you to see and you see a bloody, wet, ugly looking alien. Do not freak out; after the initial shock, the drugs will kick in and it will be a magical moment where you too will remember your baby looked beautiful. I did not even have any drugs and I thought my little, white, gooey slimy alien was cute.

They will make your baby cry and start drying it off in a fast and almost abusive looking way. They may suction its mouth and nose and almost immediately start giving it grades, called an APGAR score at one and five minutes of age. To hear most parents talk about their baby's scores you would think they were the equivalent to an IQ test. The baby is given one to two shots, wrapped up in some blankets, given back to Mom and Dad for awhile to bond with and then whisked away to the mysterious nursery. This nursery must be a very magical place, because the baby will come back looking clean, pink, very cute, and probably very hungry. Now you look back and wonder…what just happened?

Let us go through the previous scenario and try and explain what just happened. After the baby is born the obstetrician will hand the baby to a nurse or pediatrician who now will have the primary responsibility of taking care of the baby. The days of holding a baby upside down and spanking its booty until it cries are long gone, but we do try and stimulate the baby to cry...this will be its first breath. (I personally think popping their little butt to start off life may be what's missing in the discipline of today's youth and we should blame pediatricians for all the out of control teenagers). If the baby has passed stool prior to being born you will hear the term meconium stained fluid. (Meconium is a fancy medical word for black baby poop). If the amniotic fluid is meconium stained they will try and suction the baby's throat below the level of the vocal cords prior to it crying and taking its first breath. Your OB/Gyn may do this when the baby's head comes out. After the baby takes its first breath there will be a flurry of activity where they are rapidly drying the baby off in what looks kind of a rough way. They are trying to dry the baby as quickly as possible, because the baby is losing a lot of heat while wet and therefore a bunch of energy. At the same time, they are stimulating it to cry. If the baby does not start crying with the rubbing they will flick the bottom of their feet. (We may have given up on spanking but we're still annoying). They will also try to get a little hat on the baby to cover its head and get it under a warmer as soon as possible. In amongst the drying and warming up they will be listening to heart sounds and the baby's lungs to make sure everything sounds good. They will also assess APGAR scores at one and five minutes after birth. This is a score given in five different categories; each receives a score of zero to two. The five categories are then added together to get an APGAR score. These scores are a way for medical personnel to communicate to each other what the baby looked like at these times. The scores are used to give an idea of how well or how poorly the baby looked and responded at specific times right after birth. The first of the two shots given is a Vitamin K shot; an essential vitamin babies may be deficient in that allows blood to clot and thus keep them from bleeding excessively. The second shot would be a Hepatitis B shot if you had given them permission to start this vaccine series while in the hospital. They will probably at the time they are giving shots put some ointment into the baby's eyes. This is to prevent any possibility of the baby getting an infection in the eyes, which is a cause of blindness in babies.

While the baby is in the nursery the nurses do a much more thorough assessment and get the baby's vital signs. They may take the baby's length, weight, and head measurements or they may have done them in the room after they were born. They will get the baby's footprint for its birth certificate and give it a bath. After the baby's bath they will keep it under a warmer to get it warm and will keep it until it can maintain its temperature. Most hospitals have gone to mother baby rooms, which mean the mother and baby will stay together throughout the hospital stay, and as soon as the baby is doing well they are taken back to Mom's room for her to feed. After that the babies will spend most of their time in the room with Mom and Dad so they can take care of their little tyke. Just a little warning for Dad; those chairs that convert to a bed for you to sleep on were invented by a woman who evidently just had a very bad birthing experience. They were especially designed to cause pain everywhere, tempting you with the idea of blissful sleep only to cruelly prevent it happening.

Depending on the type of delivery you have, you may stay between 24 hours to three to four days in the hospital. You will probably have lots of visitors, take some naps, and get some help from nurses and doctors and then go home where everything changes when you are all alone.

Here are a couple of little tips for your time in the hospital that you might not have known. If they open something for your baby but do not use it all—diapers, wipes, ointment or the like—take it home with you. You were charged for the whole container not just what you used. By law you have the right to stay 48 hours in the hospital for a vaginal delivery and 72 hours for an uncomplicated cesarean section. Hospitals sometimes try and rush you out; do not let them if you are not ready to go. Everyone who talks to you in the hospital is not an expert. Lactation consultants sometimes are pushy and only see one side of things and this could be a side that does not always agree with how you need to live your life. Nurses sometimes give advice based on their experience and not necessarily based on scientific facts. If you have questions it is best to ask your doctors.

Here's a funny little anecdote from the hospital when my oldest boy was born, showing you crazy things even happen to pediatricians. I was on call when his mom went into the hospital and I am known for not exactly dressing the part of a normal doctor. I had on a pair of blue jeans, a t-shirt and tennis shoes and was wearing a motorcycle jacket with Wildman written across the back and a Tasmanian devil. I kept getting paged while we were in the hospital room so I would go to the corner where I could get reception on my cell phone and return the calls. One nurse, who saw me go to the corner a couple of times, turned to me angrily and said, "You can stop dealing drugs long enough for your baby to be born." I pointed out I was a doctor and on call. Another nurse pointed out that mommy was also a doctor and worked in the hospital. The first nurse apologized and we did not see her anymore.

Kaden's logs

August 19, 2011

It was a day, a day like any other day, except for me, because it was a day like no other day. Today was Kaden's birth day.

So the day started off kind of odd because it was a Friday and I did not get up at 5:30 a.m. to go to work (I didn't wake up at 5:30 a.m. and slap a snooze button until 6:30 a.m. like I am prone to do.). When I did get up I did the normal shower and dress thing until it hit me that today was the big birth day for our new little one. At that moment I knew I needed to do an activity...any activity to make me not do back flips (not a good idea as I'm pretty sure I would have put myself in the hospital), so I started putting a crib together. Before you start making comments about my lack of preparation for a baby's arrival, you should know we have a bassinet, snuggler, crib, and vibrating sleeper already put together and this was a truly unneeded item. As I was getting close to done the word came down the stairs, "It is time to go to the hospital."

I get the two of us in the car with the stuff that has been packed for the last two days. I start driving to Parkwest Hospital and then I start this deep breathing activity. I try to diagnose myself... Kussmaul breathing? No, I haven't had a head trauma. Could it be asthma or anaphylaxis? No, I don't have asthma or allergies. I must be having a panic attack. I try to go to my happy place with the flowing stream and the flowers blooming, but it just makes me need to pee. We get to the hospital and get to our room. I'm like a cat on crack! While I'm going down to the car for another load of stuff I am warned by one of the nurses I know very well that I need to calm down because I'm going to make Kristi nervous. I decide to go say "Hi" to a couple of my families who happen to be delivering at the same hospital which I'm pretty sure convinced them I was a cat on crack.

We go to the OR for the C-section and let me just say it is a totally different experience setting in the little stool by the mommy's head than it is catching the baby and drying him off. I manage to take the worst newborn picture ever and mass text it to my friends and family proving I am a total moron, but at least I manage not to drop the phone. I start getting texts from family telling me the baby in the worst *looking picture ever taken looks just like me. Lucky for him he looks better when he's completely dried off and given a bath. I think he will eventually have a chance with the ladies. During the course of the afternoon I manage to lose my phone twice, my keys twice, Kristi's phone at least once and send some nonsensical texts. I go to the car and bring up the 60 dollars worth of "It's a boy" chocolate stuff we had forgotten, only to find $60 worth of stuff the consistency of runny dog poop.*

It has been great day! Kaden is cute in spite of his dad. Kristi is doing well, in spite of my jokes. The staff has treated us great. We have a new member of our family and because of the fact I am sometimes a ditz he will have some funny stories about his big day. Happy birth day Kaden Whitten James.

August 20, 2011

My name is Kaden James and this is my first day of life. I will be one day old in about three hours and it has been a very full day so far. First off I would like to complain about being rudely jerked out of my mommy. I was just taking a little swim in my hot tub when Dr. Yang rudely pulled me out and then showed my wet naked body off to half the nation. Before I was clean, bathed or dressed I had my picture taken by my daddy who quickly sent it out around the country and has quite possibly ruined my social life for the foreseeable future.

My parents seem OK, but they keep staring at me with silly smiles. They don't seem to quite have my feeding down. Mom goes to feed me, which seems very warm and comfortable and I like to go to sleep but I'm still very hungry. Daddy takes over with a bottle, which is not nearly as snuggly and warm but I do get some food. It would be nice if the two of them could somehow combine the two. This diaper thing is quite a pain. I would be more than happy to just sit on the toilet if they would just listen to me tell them I have to go because I just don't think I can say it any plainer... you would think they would have at least learned some babyese prior to inviting me out of my warm hot tub. Instead they wrap me up in this wad of paper and plastic and expect me to pee and poop all over myself. They are somehow, astonished by the mess I make, and this is embarrassing.

Finally, I would like to complain about that Dr. Yang again. She took me to a little closet room and proceeded to whack my parts. I had just been admiring it and thinking about its possible uses and potential and she proceeded to whack about a third of it off. I feel like some of my dreams have been cut short.... literally.

These parents may have potential so I won't give up on them just yet. I've already trained them to jump at my command, they may yet deliver in the food department, and if I can just get them to stop that silly smiling thing we will get along just fine.

CHAPTER 8

Oh my God, what have we done?
(the first few days home)

Those first few days home you will be sure the hospital forgot to
send something home with you.

Well, you are now home and you are ready to relax after the craziness of the hospital, delivery, all the visitors, and not sleeping in your own bed. You think getting home is comparable to the best vacation in the whole world...then you realize you had to bring the baby home with you and your home will never be the same again. The world of parenthood was kind of delayed by being in the hospital with nurses to help, visitors to help, and a nursery was at least an option to use. Now it is just the two of you and a **BABY** (cue eerie music).

Do not freak out, (everyone freaks out) everything will be fine (it is never fine). There are going to be a couple of changes your baby is going to go through these first few days you are totally unprepared for, thus this chapter. We will just try to go through things systematically.

Eating: The baby is starting to eat more and you are not sure how much it should eat. It should eat every two and a half to three hours and will take anywhere from one and a half ounces to three ounces each time. Breastfed babies will eat 15-20 minutes on each side. Babies do not always know when they are full and will sometimes eat until they spit up. If you have increased the amount you are feeding them and they start spitting up they are just too full. Yes, it is OK if the spit-up comes out their nose. If their mouth is closed it is going to shoot out both nostrils. (Gross).

Breastfeeding: If you are wondering if your breast milk has come in yet, it has not. There is nothing subtle about breast milk coming in. You will feel like you have become a dairy and will be leaking milk every time the baby cries or it is close to feeding time. By now your nipples may be getting a little sore. You may even start to see a little cracking and some bleeding. This is when you need to be strong and the painful part will pass in the next week. Make sure you are using the good positioning the lactation consultants taught you in hospital. Make sure you are breaking suction when taking the baby off the breast. Rub a little expressed breast milk on your nipples after the baby is done and it will help heal any rawness happening. Watch for excessive redness, excessive pain or sudden swelling of your breast as this can indicate an infection known as mastitis. If you have any of these get a hold of your obstetrician as soon as possible.

Pooping: The baby has gotten through the black, tarry meconium and is now passing yellowish-green, loose stools and may be pooping every time they eat. It is completely normal for them to have from zero to 12 stools per day. If by this stage your baby has not had a dirty diaper in three days you should call your pediatrician. If they are having over 12 stools per day or passing hard balls you should also give them a call. Make sure you try to change the baby as soon as possible when they fill their drawers or they will develop a nasty diaper rash.

Peeing: Your baby should have at least four wet diapers in 24 hours. This may be hard to tell with all the poop. This is most important to watch in breastfed babies who are at risk of getting dehydrated while waiting for Mom's breast milk to come in. Their urine can range from clear to yellow to dark greenish-yellow depending on the baby's fluid intake. Sometimes in the first couple of days you may see some orange colored urine on the diaper. These are urate crystals and are caused from getting a little dehydrated and should go away once the baby is eating better and peeing more.

Skin: Your baby may develop a diaper rash from their bazillion poopy diapers. This is usually just skin irritation and you just need to put diaper rash cream on in a thick layer and change those diapers when they are dirty. A very common newborn rash shows up now, it is red blotches moving all over and sometimes they have little yellow centers. This is called erythema toxicum and can last the first couple of weeks of life. There is nothing you did to cause this and nothing to make it go away. It is very common for a baby's skin to peel especially if they were born on time or late. The only problem ever happening with this is sometimes they peel so deeply you may see a little bleeding at their wrists and ankles. It is fine to use baby lotion to help moisten up their skin.

Noises: That really loud annoying sound they make is called a cry and it happens for all kinds of reasons. The most common reasons are because the baby is hungry, wet, dirty, sleepy, has a bellyache because it did not get burped well enough, wants to be held, does not want to be held, or is just ticked off at the world because you took it out of its warm cuddly belly and are now exposing it to the cold, harsh world. Try to remain calm while assessing your baby's cries. They can pick up on your stress and it just makes them worse. Go through the list of reasons above and you will figure out which one is causing the problem. You will figure the crying out after a few days, because it will start to follow a pattern.

You have finally got ready for bed and the baby is asleep, but now it is making this terrible congested snoring sound. You are scared to death and are sure they are having problems breathing and will stop breathing and die if you do not hover over them and watch them all night long (this is freaking out by the way). This sound is caused by the fact your house is probably dry from central heat and air and it dries out the mucous inside their noses. This makes this snorty sound as they breathe in and out. It is completely normal and it does not bother them at all, it just scares you.

You just calmed yourself down about the snorty sound from above and are just about to fall asleep when you notice they are taking these five-second pauses in their breathing and then they take a few very rapid breaths. Now you know you cannot sleep and you must dedicate your lives to a revolving sleeping plan to watch the baby sleep (again freaking out). This is called periodic breathing of the newborn and is completely normal and I swear is just there to see if you are paying attention to your baby. The pauses will last about five seconds or so and then they will take three or four rapid breaths. Now if the pause lasts longer than 15 seconds you need to talk to your doctor and if it lasts longer than 20 seconds this is apnea and you need to get to the emergency department as soon as possible.

You have somehow survived the night but now your baby is hiccupping and is not very happy about it. This is also very normal and chances are they had hiccups before they were even born. A greedy baby swallowing too hard usually causes hiccups or she has had some reflux part of the way up her esophagus. Do not worry as it will go away and the baby will eventually get better at swallowing and it will not happen nearly as often.

Movements: You notice just as they are going to sleep their arms and legs jump, or it may happen when they are scared by a sudden noise or movement. You may even notice if you tap their foot their foot starts jerking a couple of times. You start to wonder if this is this a seizure? (Freak out time). It is completely normal and is called myoclonus. This is not normal in older people and can be a sign of neurological problems, but it is just caused by an immature nervous system in a baby and will go away as they get bigger.

Umbilical cord: The umbilical cord looked so easy to take care of in the hospital. Now it is all hard and shriveled and hard to clean around. How a cord gets cared for is going to vary from doctor to doctor. The base of the cord will get kind of gooey as it gets closer to falling off and this is when I recommend applying some rubbing alcohol to help it dry up. If you see any redness around the umbilical cord or if it has a foul smell, you need to talk to your pediatrician.

Sleep: They are sleeping a lot right now and some parents will think they are sleeping too much. The problem seems to be they just do not sleep when we want to be sleeping. It is not unusual for them to sleep about half of the day if you added all the time up. **<u>ALWAYS HAVE THEM SLEEP ON THEIR BACKS OR SIDES!!!</u>** It has been proven since we started having babies sleep this way the amount of SIDS (sudden infant death syndrome or crib death) has decreased by over half. This is one area you definitely want to ignore your parents, and grandparents' advice. When they tell you babies slept better on their belly, ask them how many families they knew who lost a baby to crib death. Their answer should end the discussion.

Temperature: I get several questions from parents about what temperature the house should be for the baby. I am sure this is just a husband and wife dispute over where the thermostat should be set and they want a doctor to tell the other parent their temperature is the correct one. Since I am a guy, I usually tell them the correct temperature is whatever Dad is comfortable at since Mom is hormonal (I just made that up so the guys get to win one argument in this whole parenting game.) There is not a correct temperature to keep the house. We do know babies have a harder time maintaining their body temperature than larger children or adults do. Because of this, they usually need one more layer than an adult does—this can be an extra layer of clothes or a blanket. If a baby gets cold you will notice their hands and feet turn a purple color. The purple color is because the blood flow is decreasing to their hands in order to prevent heat loss through their skin.

Senses: You have figured out they can taste, because they like to eat. They have a good sense of smell; because they can smell Mom enter the room if she is breastfeeding. They can hear and you will know this by them jumping when they hear noises. They can see, but not very far. Here in the beginning they can only see about 12 inches or so. They do like to look at faces, so get real close. They have developed a sense of touch and love being touched, so feel your baby. Touch their smooth skin, check out all their little parts, feel their silky hair. These are the ways you play and love a newborn.

Tricks: Sure other people may call these reflexes, but your baby can do some really cool tricks already. They have a grasp reflex which allows them to hold your finger if you put it in their hand (the same reflex makes them curl their toes if you touch their foot). They have a startle reflex making them jump when they hear a noise. They have a Moro reflex so if you stroke their cheek they will move their mouth toward your finger. My favorite trick is making them "dance". If you run your finger up the side of their back their bottom will curl up toward the stroked side making them "boogie".

Safety: The things you need to do to keep your baby safe are simple and will be the same for quite awhile. Make sure they are in the car seat facing backwards. Make sure your smoke detectors are working. Make sure everyone is washing his or her hands before holding your baby. **Do not smoke or let anyone smoke around your baby**!

PANIC!!! There are things to panic about and if you see them you need to seek medical attention immediately. These include the following scenarios: Your baby has a fever with a temperature above 100.4 F (do not give anything to them to make the fever go down, just get to a doctor). Your baby starts forcefully vomiting (this can be a sign of an intestinal blockage, meningitis, or bacterial infection). You cannot wake your baby up, or they are very difficult to get to eat. Your baby is having a seizure and is shaking their arms and legs. You see any bleeding from anywhere and you do not know of any trauma (except for some seepage of blood around the umbilical cord). Any of these could be signs of serious infection and need to be addressed immediately.

Hate: No, you really do not hate your partner and neither of you have been nearly as bad as what you think they have been. You are sleep-deprived, stressed out, and in Mom's case hormonally attacked. It may be time to call in the troops. This is when those pain in the neck mother in laws come in handy. Let them oooh and gooo over the baby for a few hours and get a little uninterrupted, guilt free sleep without worrying about every noise your little tadpole makes. They will be safe with Grandma for a little while...right...OK you are right sleep is not important.

Calm down: All the things you have read and heard do not always happen. All the things people said you had to do...you do not have to. Babies do not follow rules or books. No baby has ever blown up from not burping. They have never cried so hard their head blows up. They have never starved to death because you did not feed them every three hours on the dot. Remember the world of babies is not black and white, it is mostly gray. Go with the flow, and trust your instincts. If you are worried, call your doctor, the worst thing that could happen is they tell you everything is OK and at least it will calm you down.

Just a little anecdote of my own personal, "OMG what have I done?" moments. Dalton was born on New Year's Eve and we got to take him home on January 2 and it was freezing cold. I had made one trip to the car to take stuff down and had come back to the room to get the last of the stuff. I gathered up everything and told them to take Tina and Dalton down to the front door and I would pick them up. When I got to the car to put the stuff in I realized I did not have any car keys. I looked in the car and there they were on the floor. I had dropped them while I was installing the car seat into the car. I found a phone and called security. It took them 30 minutes to get to the car and another 15 minutes to get the door unlocked. Did I happen to mention I had left my coat in the car so I would not have as much stuff to carry? By the time I got into the car I was completely frozen and by the time I got to the front door neither of my two passengers was very happy with me. Stuff can happen to anyone…even the people who do this for a living.

Kaden's logs

August 21, 2011

It has been a busy 24 hours. I have learned several life lessons and have figured out things about my family. First my life lessons:

1. *If I contract the muscles of my bladder with approximately 22lbs/in pressure while simultaneously releasing the constrictor muscles of my urethral meatus and aiming my penis at 12 degrees, I will pee in my own face. If I repeat the same experiment with an angle of 35 degrees I will pee in a nurse's face. I will stick with the second set of vectors as I have found the result a lot funnier than the first.*

2. *I can poop a bunch. I took in about 24 ounces of fluid in the last 24 hours, give or take a wet burp or two, and I have managed to poop a mountain of dirty diapers. The approximate weight of said diapers is about 40 pounds. Given the fact I only weigh six lbs. six oz. I have managed to already disprove one of the basic physic staples that matter cannot be made or destroyed. Suck on that Sir Isaac Newton! Forgive me if I've referenced the wrong science nerd—I'm only two days old!*

3. *I have made my first medical diagnosis. I'm pretty sure my daddy has ADHD, but do not fear I have also figured out how to cure him. After sleep deprivation of about 34 hours he is completely cured. Unfortunately it seems to be short-lived since he got five to six hours of sleep and it returned.*

4. *I am cute, people let down their guard around cute people, and it is up to me to take over the world while I am still cute. People keep saying I*

look like my daddy. I have seen my daddy. I know I have a very short window to use my cute factor to my advantage.

Things I've observed:

1. *My mommy is the prettiest cyborg on the planet. I know she is part human because she is soft and sweet. I know she is part machine because she has wires and tubes and makes beeping noises all the time.*

2. *My daddy's eyes will cross at about the 34th hour of sleep deprivation point and Mommy's do it about two hours later.*

3. *Everyone wants me to look like him or her. I would like to pick and choose my parts. Have you seen the feet on my daddy? Thank goodness mine came from Mommy!*

4. *I must have a pretty nice Mommy and Daddy because there have sure been a bunch of people checking on them.*

Of special note, I am currently writing my manifesto and I have put out my first warning video about my upcoming world domination. I don't know the exact time-line, but it has to happen before I look too much like Daddy.

August 23, 2011

My fourth day of life and I continue in my quest of self-awareness. I am pretty sure I am meant to be a super hero. I have all the makings of the classic hero: great looks...check, amazing physique...check, cool secret lair...check (my bedroom rocks and I'm pretty sure there are gators in my moat), and super powers...check. I'm still exploring all the options of my powers and have made a few discoveries about them.

First I have some mystical powers. I have already written about how I can violate the laws of physics with the sheer volume of poop I am capable of making. I have also learned I can teleport my pee. So far I have managed to get my pee to wet the entire bed and while keeping my diaper completely dry. That skill in itself was pretty amazing to me, but there is more. I can summon food with my mind. All I have to do is think that I am hungry and make a little squeak and food magically appears. Food must give me some strange power as well since after eating I can make a large noise that exits my mouth and can make my surroundings vibrate. I am sure I have other powers I have not yet discovered, but I will; after all I am only on my fourth day.

I do have some archenemies already. I do not like clothing, but I also do not like nakedness. There seem to be people who have learned this already and try and alter-

nate me from one to the other, causing me great discomfort. I also have a weakness: if I am tightly wrapped in a blanket I will fall instantly asleep. I'm thinking with the proper costume I can combat the first weakness so I will stay constantly vigilant for people with blankets.

I could use some help with just a couple of minor details in my quest for world domination via super herodom. I need a cool super-hero name and a cool costume. Feel free to send me any suggestions. With the costume please remember I have reddish brown hair that shouldn't clash and I will need some extra room in the crotch section for my large diaper bulge.

Well I am off to start protecting the house. Oh no! A blanket ... ZZZZZZZZZZZZZZZZZZ!

August 25, 2011

Today I had to go to my first doctor's visit. It wasn't as bad as I thought it could have been. My prostrate did not have to get checked and I didn't have to get a colonoscopy done and there weren't any shots. After that it went straight downhill. As soon as I went through the door they took my clothes off. If you have read my previous logs you will know this is not my favorite thing in life. They weighed me and I gained some weight (this is a good thing because whoever heard of a six pound superhero?) I was measured and I am a good distance away from two feet (maybe my superhero power will be to stretch otherwise I will be staring down villains at their ankles and I don't even have any teeth to be an ankle biter). A doctor examined me and he told my parents I was perfect. I, on the other hand, would like to inform him that his hands were cold and his jokes could use some sharpening. Lots of ladies came into the room and said I was a good baby and looked like my daddy (sure hoping that goatee comes in fast). I will need to learn some jokes, do some magic tricks and develop a sparkling personality if I'm going to get anywhere with the ladies. It was a stressful day so when I got home I hit the bottle pretty hard and passed out.

CHAPTER 9

The longest month of your life (birth to one month of age)

There will come a time this month that all sounds waking you up
will sound the same, and you will just want them to stop.

Just to be honest with each other this is going to be a tough month. The only reason you will be able to get through this month and ever have another child is because the shock and sleep deprivation will cause you to forget most of it. This chapter cannot really give you great insight into how to make this better, but at least you will know you are not alone and the people saying they had a great first month are suffering from that shock thing or are just lying.

Peeing: You will become an expert in changing diapers and clothes in this month. A baby is going to typically go through six to 12 diapers a day, many of these accompanied by a clothing change that include both you and the baby (especially when you're changing a little boy with a fire hose). This is when you will find out little boys will get an erection when they have to pee (yes it is normal). You will also learn to duck and cover if you see a twitch of their penis (you will see what I mean when you get doused). It is a little twitch that happens right before they let loose a stream and gives you a chance to put the diaper over them and protect yourself and everything around you. You will find even with little girls that have no hose they can sure make quite a fountain. Unfortunately they do not give you any warning before showering everything. It is my theory that this first month they think we need practice changing diapers, because it seems like they always save some to pee on the new diaper just as we are putting it on.

Pooping: They seem to have an endless supply of poop. They are eating more and their gastro-colic reflex (a reflex that makes them poop when their stomach is full) is in full swing. Poop will vary in color and consistency and should not worry you much except about how to pay for all the diapers and wipes you are going through. Call your pediatrician if you see poop which is red or black, or is coming out as hard balls. As we get close to a month old it is not unusual for the amount of dirty diapers to start slowing down, but they may get larger in amount per time. As this reflex goes away you will see your baby start to strain, cry, turn red and pass a lot of gas. This is not a problem with milk or with gas it is just normal. They will figure out how to poop in a couple of weeks and this will all pass. Do not change formulas and do not buy gas drops, you will just be wasting your money.

Some laws of physics seem to be violated by the amount of matter exiting a baby.

Eating: They seem to eat all the time. If you are breastfeeding you will feel like you are connected to a baby all the time. The reason you feel that way is because you are attached to your baby all the time. If you are bottle feeding you may have less time feeding, but you will find you are getting to know your dishwasher too well because there are always bottles to be washed. Your baby only needs milk to eat. Do not give them any solid foods no matter what your friends and family tell you. It will not cause them to sleep longer and it can cause constipation. Adding solid food to a baby's diet has been found to increase their chances of developing food allergies, eczema and asthma. It can also lead to babies with bellyaches and fussiness (something you do not need any more of).

Hate #1: Your relationships will become a little strained; you may even hate each other a little. Mom is tired and hormonal. Dad is tired, feels a little lonely (after all he was the highlight of Mom's life before J.R. arrived) and a little stressed (guys do not handle crying women very well). You both may feel the other person should be doing more because it seems like you are doing so much. The reason it feels that way is because there is a lot more that needs to be done. This is usually the time you are going to have some good fights. Remember you are tired, hormonal and stressed out so be nice. Neither one of you will handle the little urchin well completely on your own, ask any single parent.

Hate #2: Ignore your friends and family. This is the time where you learn where all the horror stories about in-laws come from. They will want to see you more that probably will just use some time you could have taken a nap, done dishes, shopped or done laundry. They will give you useless advice you either already figured out or is just wrong. Take every secret or tip they want to give you with a grain of salt. If it sounds stupid, it is. If it sounds too good to be true, it is. Use them when it benefits you but only if it benefits you. Do not let anyone guilt you into anything at this time, you are already doing the most important thing you can do…taking care of your baby.

This month your baby is the most vulnerable to illness. I recommend babies stay away from crowded places like stores, church and restaurants. Any place where there are more than a couple people (especially children), in a closed place you will be exposing your baby to illnesses. We worry about any temperature above 100.4 in a baby who is less than two months old. Most babies who develop a fever are put in the hospital and have what is called a septic workup with blood tests, a urine test and a test of their spinal fluid with IV antibiotics for 48 hours. The chances of your baby getting sick go down the more careful you are. Make sure everyone washes his or her hands before holding your baby. If someone is sick keep them away from your baby. Mild illnesses in adults can be life threatening in a newborn baby.

Sleep: Sleeping is something you may think you are not getting enough of, but you have probably had some questions about your baby's sleep. A baby will sleep anywhere between 12-18 hours a day. They pretty much wake up just to pee, poop, and eat. They have no schedule this first month and day and night mean nothing to them. It is important to wake your baby up to eat every three to four hours in the beginning until your baby starts gaining weight. When your baby starts gaining weight you just let them eat when they want to. Remember your baby should be sleeping on their back or side all the time.

Safety: At each visit your pediatrician will tell you what things you need to do or be worried about to keep your baby safe. In the first month this will include having your baby sit in the car seat facing backwards in the back seat. The safest spot is the middle of the seat, but if some reason they cannot sit in the middle the next safest place is the passenger side. A baby can only sit in the front seat if you have no back seat and have disabled the passenger side's airbag. Make sure all the smoke detectors in the house are working and have fresh batteries. Make sure the hot water heater in the house is turned down to economy or 120 degrees. This is still hot enough to get everything done but won't scald your baby. This is most important before your baby becomes a toddler but you will not have time to do it then. Make sure you have a thermometer because any temperature above 100.4 is an emergency and your baby needs to be seen immediately by a doctor. Stay away from crowded places and make sure everyone is washing their hands.

Tricks: You will discover a few things your baby can do this month. If you are breastfeeding your baby can smell its mommy and find her in a crowded room. They will jump when they hear a loud noise. They can burp like a sailor and pass gas like a frat boy. I have had parents tell me their baby can say Mama or Dada (they were delusional from lack of sleep). Their best trick is how a crying, burping, poop factory can totally wear out two very healthy, energetic adults. They will start to look around more and start to have a little bit of a personality. They will be kicking and squirming a lot, which is always fun to watch.

Panic: The things to panic about have not really changed from the first couple of days. Your baby has a fever with a temperature above 100.4 F (do not give anything to make the fever go down just get to a doctor). Your baby starts forcefully vomiting (this can be a sign of an intestinal blockage, meningitis, or bacterial infection). You cannot wake your baby up, or it's very difficult to get them to eat. Your baby is having a seizure and is shaking their arms and legs.

For some of the common little problems that shows up this first month and their signs and symptoms see chapter 20. You may start to see constipation, colic, cradle cap, gastroesophageal reflux, milk intolerances, neonatal congestion and of course the illnesses babies can get at any age. These are the things your pediatrician is here for…make them earn their money.

Checkup: It is now time to go to the doctor for your baby's month old checkup. Make a list of everything you want to ask your doctor. They are going to weigh and measure your baby and give you an idea how big they are compared to everybody else. They will ask what kind of milk they are drinking, how much and how often. They will ask how often they are peeing and pooping. They will go over safety stuff and things to look for. They will look your baby over from head to toe and point out anything they see that might be different or will need to be watched. The baby might get their Hepatitis B #2 shot at this visit depending on what type of vaccines they are using. Your doctor will then tell you what to expect in the next month...you will forget everything they told you...therefore the next chapter exists as a reminder of the things they told you about.

Kaden's logs

August 31, 2011

Today I am 12 days old. My mommy and daddy took me to the office and I weigh 7 lbs. and I am 20 inches long. I'm not really bragging but I am really cut...ladies eat your heart out I only have love for my mommy. Today I am going to talk about something that every southern boy, and most of the girls, knows something about. We are going to talk about pit stops.

I have my own personal pit crew called Mommy and Daddy. I am pretty sure Mommy is the pit chief. She controls the food source and is the director of the traffic. Daddy is more the flunky. When I decide it is time for a pit stop during the nighttime race here at the James' speedway, I signal the crew by three grunts, a stretch and then a belier (southern talk for a loud scream). The pit chief then signals the flunky it's time to transport me to the pit by a quick elbow to the lower ribs. Daddy then jumps out of bed like a lightening bolt. There are times I need the tires changed (diaper), sometimes the wiper fluid leaks (Daddy gets peed on or my clothes get wet) and I need some fresh paint (clothes), then I'm off to Mommy for a quick fuel up. It is at this juncture that my pit stop grinds to a stop. It seems to take about 30 minutes for a fuel-up. I can tell my pit crew would like this to be faster, but we evidently need more practice. We have heard rumors of pit stops that lasted as little as 15 minutes but it is not happening at this speedway. We have also heard of night races occurring without a single pit stop. I think my crew is hoping to get to that point.

The pit crew is improving and I don't think I'm going to fire anyone just yet. In another couple of months I think we will be able to compete with any other team out there.

September 2, 2011

I am two weeks old today. Man, my parents feel a lot older today. I have sure learned a bunch of stuff in my first two weeks. Here is a summation of my vast amount of knowledge:

1.   *Mommy and Daddy need at least five hours of sleep a day or their eyes look funny.*

2.   *I hate poop! I will cry very loud if poop touches my bottom. If this happens at night it may mean Mommy and Daddy get less than five hours of sleep.*

3.   *Dieting is no big deal... If my Mommy can lose 25 pounds in 13 days, what's my Daddy's problem?*

4.   *My Daddy says that I give the hiccups to myself because I'm a greedy baby. All I know is when I have the hiccups I'm a ticked off baby. I guess I am mad at myself.*

5.   *As I eat more food I tend to poop more and it also takes me longer to eat. This leads to Mommy and Daddy getting less sleep.*

6.   *If you are a boy you should not go see an OB/GYN. They will take out a sharp knife and try and turn you into a girl.*

7.   *I am cute and people like to tell me so. My Mommy and Daddy spend hours staring at me and telling me I'm cute. If they would spend a little less time staring at me they might get some sleep.*

8.   *I believe parents are happier if they have a date night. I let my parents have dates at night usually around 1:00 a.m. and 4:00 a.m. They always give each other a kiss and their eyes cross because they are so in love.*

9.   *Babies bring families together. We have had lots of family come see us and we have even more coming in the next several weeks.*

10.   *Diapers are a significant contributor to landfill and I am doing my bit.*

11.   *My daddy thought diaper wipe warmers were a waste of money before I was born. My mommy did not believe him and bought one anyway. My daddy still thinks it is a waste of money.*

12.   *Evidently if your parents don't get enough sleep they will try to drown you. My parents have tried to drown me twice so far. Sure I smell good but I'm trying to avoid it in the future.*

13. *My daddy is a terrible carpenter. The word "crap" means, "I've drilled those holes in the wrong spot".*

14. *Blinds.com is a great place to get blinds from when your daddy is a terrible carpenter since they will replace screw-ups.*

15. *My mommy has sexy feet and ankles when she loses 25 pounds.*

16. *When you get old you lose pieces and parts. I have lost my electric cord that plugged me into Mommy. I guess I am solar powered now. I am hoping the government sends me a Green Energy Grant.*

17. *No matter how hard I chew on my daddy he will not breastfeed.*

18. *My mommy is colorblind. She said my hair was brown, Daddy said it was red. Daddy was right. From now on Daddy should get to make all the color decisions around the house.*

19. *Shots suck...I'm just saying.*

20. *I have learned that even though I have only loved my family for two weeks it feels like I have loved them my whole life. (Did you get it?)*

September 12, 2011

Today's log is all about a little R-E-S-P-E-C-T so sock it to me now.

Today was a little lesson in respect for my daddy to respect all my mommy does for me. Daddy is a little too full of himself about what a great Daddy and what a great husband he is to Mommy. Every once in a while he needs to be brought down a peg or two to show him how it is. Today just happened to be one of those days.

Mommy had to take big brother Tyler to football practice. That left Daddy, big brother Dalton and I to fend for ourselves (well Daddy to fend for both of us). We got home at 6:00 p.m. and I decided to try and blow my main vein. I was starving because it had been a whole hour and a half since I had last eaten. Daddy somehow managed to get us in the house and shakily make me a bottle, which I promptly devoured. Daddy had plans to impress my mommy with his abilities to get some stuff done around the house like laundry and straightening up in general, you know the drill. After I had eaten my food I felt a full diaper was in order, so Daddy changed me. Then Dalton was hungry and needed food, but what to feed him? Well it took Daddy a little too long to contemplate that so I decided to pee all over my new diaper and my clothes. Daddy took me to my room and changed my diaper and clothes. I decided at that point it had been about an hour since I last ate and it was time to eat again. Daddy made another bottle and I ate it as well and then decided to poop. Daddy again changed my diaper. By this time my brother Dalton was starving so Daddy put me in my lamb seat and set me up on the counter while preparing a gourmet meal for him and Dalton. The peanut butter and jelly sandwiches and Doritos were quickly wolfed down and Daddy decided to do some laundry.

Daddy got the laundry out of the drier when I decided to eat again. It was my third bottle since 6 p.m. and it was only 8 p.m. Daddy got Dalton to help him feed me while he quickly folded some laundry. Mommy finally got home and saved my daddy, who, by this time, had lost at least 50 hairs off his head, developed indigestion and a nervous twitch.

Daddy learned that Mommy is the MAN! and he can't handle the HOUSE. Daddy is a better team player than a soloist. Mommy can do it all on her own. Mommy needs some RESPECT. I recommend Daddy say it with diamonds.

CHAPTER 10

What doesn't kill you makes you want to die (months 1-2)

Doctors know some of your questions are just ways to settle fights and sometimes we unfairly pick sides.

I would like to tell you the second month is easier than the first but it is not really. It may be a little better because you are better at changing diapers, dressing and feeding baby which may give you more time for those little extras like taking a shower and doing some laundry, but we still have not got to the part where you get to sleep yet.

Eating: Eating is now a routine and is much easier to plan around. By this time you can almost set your clock to when your baby is going to eat and the amount they are going to eat is mostly the same each time. If all of a sudden your baby starts eating less for more than one feeding you should wonder if there is a reason, like an illness. The one exception to this regular schedule is babies will often have a growth spurt at a month of age and may have a couple of weeks where they want to eat all the time (well at least every two hours or so). Most babies still are not able to sleep through the night but you do not need to wake them to eat. Doctors do not recommend feeding your baby anything except milk during this month (including water, juice, and any solid foods).

Sleeping: Your baby's sleeping habits will become more routine as well this month. A baby is more likely to be taking naps at regular intervals and for set periods of time. They still will not sleep through the night but their wakeful times are more routine. There is no set amount of sleep a baby will get each day and every baby will be different. The only thing you can do to make your baby's sleep patterns more predictable is to keep a very regular schedule with time to go to sleep and time to get up. Ignore your family and friends and all their helpful "cures" that cause their babies to sleep through the night. Do not give your baby anything except milk and love to fall asleep unless recommended by your doctor. A full night's sleep is not worth a dead baby.

Pooping: The baby's pooping is thankfully less than what it was the first month. Around the start of this month a baby's gastro-colic reflex goes away and they get where they may only stool once to twice a day. It is also completely normal for them not to have a dirty diaper every day. Contrary to what your grandparents thought, a baby does not have to have a dirty diaper every day to be healthy. As long as the baby's stools are not hard balls (constipation), they can go 3-4 days without having a dirty diaper. Instead of worrying about it, enjoy not having to change those stinky diapers. The color may change and may be yellow, green or brown. You should never see red or black stools and if you do you need to talk to your pediatrician. Never give your baby anything for constipation without talking to your pediatrician's office.

Peeing: You are absolutely right; they can pee all the time. The amount of pee coming out of them defies all laws of science. You are sure by this time that more pee comes out than the amount of fluid going into them. You can now change wet diapers in about two seconds and it does not require you to wake up to get the job done.

Hate: OK you two parents may have started to like each other again and figured out it is the two of you against the baby...yea that is it, you hate the baby. No, it is not right, you cannot hate the baby. You hate your parents; yes that is something the two of you can agree on. They are to blame for all your faults and they are always in the way. Oh, by the way, have I told you grandparents are my enemy? They drive me completely bonkers.

Tricks: They start to be more than just poop and pee factories this month. As we get closer to two months old they can start to smile and really mean it. That means if you are entertaining them they will reward you with a smile. They may even start to laugh at you. Their little arms and legs are going a million miles an hour and they honestly act like they know you and want you around. This is the real trick, they torture you nonstop and yet you love every inch of them. They are able to turn to locate sound. They can start to hold their head up and stop being just a large bobble head. To help out the neck strength it is time for tummy time. Just to warn you, most babies hate tummy time because they cannot hold up their head yet. It may help to get down on the floor with them and touch and talk to them while they are down there. They will eventually get enough strength to lift up their head and then it will not bother them. Their newborn reflexes start to go away at this stage and they develop the reflex when you turn their head to the side their arm points straight out on the side they are facing and the other arm bends up over their head. They look like little fencers. They know the sound of your voice and may even start to recognize their own name. They can now see several feet away and are going to start looking around more.

Safety: The safety advice from last month is the same this month. Nothing really changes. The car seat stays in the same place. The baby still is not going anywhere fast, but they are wrigglier so you want to make sure not to leave them on a changing table or couch by themselves or they may fall off. They are also going to start putting their hands in their mouth. Make sure there is nothing around them they can get a hold of and put it in their mouth to choke on. Still stay away from places there could be sick people hanging out.

Panic: We still get excited about any fevers, so if your baby has a temperature over 100.4 you need to see a doctor as soon as possible. You also need to see a doctor fairly quickly if your baby starts forcefully vomiting more than just a couple of times or starts having more than six loose stools in a day.

There are a couple of problems that may show up this month which will either concern you or need to be addressed by your pediatrician. They are colic, gastro-esophageal reflux, cradle cap, pyloric stenosis and of course other illnesses change depending on the season. A good rule of thumb is: if you are worried about something ask your doctor and not all your "doctor" friends and family.

Checkup: Boy time sure flies when you are having fun...or are sleep deprived. It is time for your baby's two-month-old checkup and this one is a doozey. This is the first of many big shot days. Your baby will be getting multiple vaccines today. The number of actual needle sticks will vary depending on what vaccines your pediatrician has chosen to use but they will be receiving vaccines for: diphtheria, tetanus, pertussis, Hemophilus, polio, streptococcus pneumonia, rotavirus, and possibly hepatitis B. Make sure you have your list of questions to ask, bring your diaper bag, a bottle would not be a bad idea to calm the baby down after the shots, and of course do not forget the baby. . It is probably a good idea to check with your pediatrician to see if they recommend giving a dose of acetaminophen after the vaccines. Ask your doctor's office for the correct dose of acetaminophen to give if they recommend it.

At the checkup your baby will be weighed, measured and plotted on a growth curve to compare their growth to the last visit. The doctor will ask you about their eating, peeing, pooping and what they are doing developmentally. They will look your baby over from head to toe and tell you about anything they find. Finally, they should go over the vaccines they will be receiving and any possible side effects you might see and what to do if you see each of them. They will also go over any problems you might have happened over the next two months until they see you again. You leave the office shaking and possibly crying because they have given your baby shots, whereas your baby is probably already asleep and has forgotten the whole thing. You may need to stop by a bar or take a nerve pill and then you will forget everything they said again, hence the need for the next chapter.

Kaden's logs

September 20, 2011

Today officially sucked. My daddy works at torture chamber called a doctor's office. Getting older isn't all it is cracked up to be.

Yesterday was my one-month birthday. There were no presents, no fanfare, and no good food; it was kind of a bummer if you ask me. Today was even worse. I was woken up early this morning and dragged to my daddy's office. It was a field trip, Mommy had a hall pass, and I was going to get looked at by some ladies and told I was handsome and such a good boy. There was some of that and then it went straight down the toilet. My parents stripped me down to my diaper. I hate being naked. They paraded me around the office, ruining my future social life yet once again. Then a doctor came into the room. Let me tell you about that pediatrician; he still has yet to learn a good joke, he has cold hands, and hasn't done a thing for me I couldn't have done for myself. He told my parents I was perfect (I knew that), said I was eating the right amount (that was a load of crap because I need my freaking steak), and said my acne was to be expected. Acne!!! I'm 32 days old, I don't need acne. This is just one more reason why I am going to take over the world and my first job will be to ban acne. He then ordered me a shot. I didn't think about it much; I've watched some TV already and figured I was just going to get my milk out of a different container when holy mackerel they proceeded to poke me in the leg with a harpoon. I screamed so loud I almost popped a vessel. My mommy then took me away from my daddy's terrible office and that evil doctor.

My daddy came home for lunch and I proceeded to tell him exactly what I thought of his office and that pediatrician and all he could say was, "Honey, he sure seems fussy." Oh brother, you don't know the half of it. I'm pretty sure my hair turned two shades darker in the red direction. Buddy, I was harpooned and I'm more than just a little mad at you and that pediatrician. I am now sleepy, but don't you think I'm not going to be torturing you both tonight. I don't have one of those harpoon things to stick you with, but I'm sure going to pee all over you when I get the chance.

September 21, 2011

On my way to entire world domination I thought I would start by bashing baby fashion. Fashion or lack thereof is something I have learned a few things about since I was born.

1. *I have a few months before I walk, therefore I don't have to wear shoes. I'm good with not wearing shoes. Since I am not wearing shoes I would also like to not wear socks. There should be no reason for my feet to get cold. If my feet are cold change the temperature of the house. The world doesn't revolve around your comfort anymore, it revolves around my wellbeing. While I'm talking about ditching the socks please get rid of the socks that look like shoes.*

2. *If you are going to wrap my butt in paper and plastic, could you at least make me look cool? I don't want silly red furry monsters; I want barbwire, outdoor scenes, camo, or a lookalike leather motorcycle jacket. It would also be nice if they didn't leak all the time. If I have to pee on myself could we at least limit the area being exposed?*

3. *There are not enough things that celebrate the close relationship I have with my daddy. I mean Daddy rocks and I want to shout that on my clothing on at least 7/10 days. I love my mommy and I like to celebrate her, but Daddy is the "MAN".*

4. *Do not put cute characters on my butt. When someone says I have a cute butt I want to know they are looking at me and not that little cock-eyed puppy.*

5. *Do not button up my shirt under my butt. There is already too much material bunched under there already. When my diaper is dirty because you made me poop and pee on myself, I sure need one more thing to slow you down like I need a hole in the head.*

6. *All baby hats are stupid. Make a fedora in my size or at least a Stetson so I can look like Papa.*

7. *Avoid clothes with stripes. I'm already under home arrest and stuck in a bed with bars, which makes me think I'm destined for a life of crime so let's limit the foreshadowing.*

8. *I am not a toy. I don't care if you think I look cute dressed up like a country gentleman, I just want something soft and roomy that has a quick exit plan.*

9. *Make the freaking head holes bigger in shirts. I'm pretty sure I am going to need those ears later in life and I'm tired of all my shirts trying to pull them off.*

10. *I think I'm about to get over my fear of naked. Let's just burn all my clothes, throw away the diapers and let me go buck-naked.*

September 29, 2011

My parents are idiots. I mean that in the nicest way but they sure do look funny. Yesterday I gave them a smile. I gave each of them a good one. They should be happy and feel content. I gave them a smile after 40 days. No, that was not enough, now they want me to smile all the time. They try to coax me to smile, beg me to smile and make stupid faces to make me smile. Then if they get me to smile (to be honest I just want a moment of peace) then they want to reward me with silly goo-goo talk to get me to do it more.

You would think with the lack of sleep they've had, and the amount of complaining they've done about the last month and a half, they wouldn't have the energy to bug me constantly. I am going to quit waking up at night for two reasons. First I'm exhausted from being forced to perform like a trained monkey all day, and second I'm a little scared that if I wake them at night to feed me they will start with the whole goo-goo, gaa-gaa crap again trying to get me to smile. If this is going to happen every time I learn something new, I am in real trouble. I think in my quest for world domination I will have to learn more skills than peeing, pooping, burping, sleeping, passing gas, occasionally spitting up on myself, and now this little smile. By the time I get myself into shape for world domination I will probably have to kill everyone in my kingdom if they utter a single goo or gaa.

CHAPTER 11

Take a deep breath there's a chance you're going to survive this whole parenthood thing (months 2-4)

Who knew that sex would some day be at the bottom of the list of things you would like to be doing?

Congratulations! You have survived to this point. I am not sure exactly what the magic of this point is, but it seems to be a monumental milestone. I tell everyone this is every parent's favorite time. I think it is due to a couple different things, not the least being you have reached bottom the last two months and there is no place to go but up. In all seriousness things do start to get better and more enjoyable. By the way, you get to sleep this month (YEAH!!!) The other little spark of interest (at least in the guy corner) is the OB/Gyn says you can start having sex again (although let's face it, those of you who really wanted to have sex have already snuck some in and the rest of you are probably too tired to care yet).

Eating: We have eating down to a science now. You can set a clock by when your little person is going to want to eat. You can make a bottle or breast-feed in your sleep now so it only makes sense that they now start sleeping through the night so you don't need to use that skill. They do not need anything besides milk to eat or drink. Still we don't give any juice, water or baby food yet. It makes the choices of what to feed them very easy…milk or milk. People are in such a hurry to give them other things to eat and drink. Enjoy the simplicity of no choices.

Peeing: They are still peeing like banshees. When you have to get all your calories to grow in liquid form you are going to be getting more fluid than you need, which means it has to come back out as pee.

Pooping: The amount of poop coming out of them is going to vary widely from baby to baby. It can go from 4-5 dirty diapers a day to only having a dirty diaper every 5-6 days (I personally like the once a week poop). People are very obsessed about their baby's poop…do not be. Only worry if the color of the poop is white, red or black. If you see any of these three colors you need to tell your pediatrician. If your baby is having poop coming out as hard balls, call your pediatrician. If your baby is suddenly having an increase in loose stools greater than six per day, call your pediatrician. Notice I say call your pediatrician and not your family or friends; go to the expert and get the right answer first.

Sleeping: This is the real section of this chapter you have been waiting for…the sleep action. You have been thinking about sleep for the last two months and now is when it gets to happen. What makes it happen? Well, at around two months of age a baby can store enough glycogen in their liver to get enough energy to go without eating for up to 12 hours at a time. HUH? No, you do not have to understand what glycogen is or how it works; you just can take my word for it that it starts to be stored better at this time of life. You still have a problem though. Your baby has been trained to wake up every three to four hours to eat. This means they come to a lighter stage of sleep every 3-4 hours. This is the time to move your baby out of your room and get them in their own room in a crib. They will still come to a lighter stage of sleep but there will not be anybody in the room snoring, snorting, moving or making noise to wake them up so they just drift back to sleep. People who listen to this advice will be rewarded by longer periods of deep restful sleep. People, who feel they cannot sleep without their baby being in the same room and close to them, will be rewarded by the continual closeness of waking up in the middle of the night to feed their baby. The baby does well either way...the parents do better when they are getting some sleep. The choice is yours to make, but if you choose the second option do not say I did not tell you so.

Hate: There are so many people to hate this month, but the nice thing is it usually is not your family. OK, so it might still be your family, but only if you hated them before you had the baby. Now is the time maternity and paternity leave has run out and you have to go to work. You get to hate the fact you have to leave your baby with someone else and you are going to miss some of the precious baby time. Of course if you get to stay at home with your baby you get to hate the people going to work having big people interaction. If someone else is caring for your baby you are going to hate at least some of the things they do with your baby or the way they do it. If you are working you are going to hate how inflexible work is about you taking time off to take your baby to the doctor or care for them being sick. You will hate the mailman...he brings all the bills that are starting to come in from the hospital. This leads to you hating your insurance company as you realize the coverage you thought you had was not exactly the coverage they are giving you. You will hate going to the store because you need a small truck to carry just the baby stuff home and you still do not have any groceries.

Safety: Read the last chapter and insert everything in here again. OK, we can also add a few more details to think about. They are going to be moving around more and may try to fall off of wherever you might be laying them so do not leave them anywhere they can do this. They now like to put everything in their mouth. Things going into the mouth are usually their fingers, fist, toes or entire foot, but if they happen to get anything in their hands, guess what...it is going into their mouth. A good rule of thumb is if it is small enough to pass through a toilet paper roll it is small enough for them to choke on. They have limited areas they can get to so make sure their area is safe. You are now out and about more so try to be safer when driving. Never leave your baby in a car alone or anywhere unattended.

Tricks: Well your baby is a little person now. She is a very messy, smelly, mute, illiterate person, but a person nonetheless. She can do some tricks leaving you amused for hours and will want to show all your friends. Try to refrain from using your baby as show-and-tell as it just lets the rest of the world know how sad your life really is. If you find your self having lengthy conversations with your friends about what your baby can do it is time for a night out with the big people...who do not have kids and do not want to hear about yours.

They can do a little more these days and are more entertaining. They will smile at you if you do just about anything in their direction. This should not be used as a time to refine your comedic chops because your baby loves you and will smile at anything you do, even stupid little baby voices and the goo-gooing gag-gagging thing you keep doing. Refrain from doing your best baby impersonation in public just to get your baby to smile; everyone has seen a baby smile and you do not need everyone thinking you're crazy— the fact your clothes are covered in spit-up, you smell like poop, its been 3-4 days since you bathed properly, and you have not done your hair or make-up since the day you went to the hospital has already convinced every-one you have lost your mind).

They can laugh. They tend to laugh with the smile, so please reread the section above and try not to go too far with this newly learned trick. Do try to take a picture of the laugh in action though because a toothless laugh on a baby is a great picture to show them what they are going to look like when they are old.

They will roll over. They do not have to roll over, but some of them will and they will pick the time when you do not want them to roll over to do it. Do not ever let go of them because they can fall off. They are just waiting for this kind of opportunity so you will never forget the first time they rolled over. It is amazing how a trip to the emergency room will for-ever be engraved in your memory.

They will say their first word. Not really, but I have many parents and grandparents who come in and swear they do. It is amazing that sometimes it is even a whole sentence like, "I love you". Parenthood is evidently like really good drugs (I mean really BAD drugs).

They can play with stuff now. Now is when the half a million toys you have already bought can start to be played with. They probably will not like them and will be fascinated by the cheapest thing you have, but they will pick things up and give them a good shake and probably smile, make googly noises and laugh that toothless laugh at them. No, do not shake the toy in public to get them to laugh either!

Panic: There is not nearly as much stuff to panic about these two months. Sure there are illnesses babies will get depending on what time of year it is, but as far as a pediatrician is concerned you have made it through the scariest time. Most of the worst things happening this month are going to be the things you do to the baby yourself. This seems to be the time people seem to drop their baby, let them fall off of things, turn a corner while carrying them and bang their head against the wall.

Checkup: Remember all those shots from the two-month visit? Well, guess what, we get to give the same ones this time. Just like last time the most common side effects you are going to see from these vaccines are going to range from nothing to being a little fussier, a little more tired and possibly less appetite. There is a small chance they may run a little low-grade fever and it is fine to give them some infant acetaminophen every 4-6 hours for fever or fussiness. Be sure to check with your doctor's office about the correct dose for your baby based on their weight. The good news is that if you do react to the vaccines, it is usually the first time you get them. The next time the reactions will be either the same or less.

Just like all the checkups you have done so far, your baby will be weighed and measured and have both plotted on a growth curve to make sure they are growing well. The doctor will ask you some developmental questions to make sure the baby is developing properly. Then they will look your baby over head to toe yet again. Do not forget your list of questions to ask the doctor. They will also go over all the things the baby will do between the four and six month checkup. Hopefully you will already know everything they tell you if I do my job right with this book and you read the next chapter before you go to your appointment.

True confessions: Here is my confession to the hurt your own baby during this time. Dalton was probably around 8-10 weeks old and had to go to the office with me one Sunday afternoon for clinic. He was sleeping peacefully in his car carrier and I was busy seeing patients. He suddenly woke up and started to cry. Now Dalton was very easy to put back to sleep or settle him down, you just had to rock him back and forth a few times. I ran out of the exam room, picked up his car carrier and gave it a few rocks. Unfortunately for Dalton his daddy had unfastened his straps so he could sleep more comfortably and I had completely forgotten I had unstrapped him as I rocked him right out of the car carrier and onto his nose and chin. His first skinned up nose and chin was due completely to me and my 2-4 month panic moment. By the way, I knew right away he was OK, but I was panicked about facing his mother and telling her how he earned his boo-boo.

Kaden's logs

October 8, 2011

Mommy and Daddy took me to the office to see how big I am today. I am 22 and a half inches long and I weigh 10 pounds. They looked back to see how big my big brothers were at this age and found I am growing more like Dalton than like Tyler. Dalton was 22 inches long and weighed 10.4 lbs. and Tyler was 24 1/2 inches long and weighed 14.6 lbs. They can compare me to them all they want to, but I'm sure I am cuter than they were. I thought we were pretty much done there at Daddy's office and then my parents started talking about illnesses and how sick Tyler had been and then the next thing I knew they stripped me down to my diaper, gave me some sugary stuff to drink and then they harpooned me... twice. I am not very happy with the two of them. I heard them tell my mommy that the most common side effects were sleepiness, decreased eating, low-grade fever and fussiness. I do admit I was kind of sleepy there for a little bit. I have eaten a bunch so they got that one wrong. I haven't had a fever yet and I don't think I want one of those. I have been a little fussy but nothing like what I have planned for my parents during the night. They will pay for harpooning each of my legs. I have not pooped in about 24 hours and I plan on letting the poop literally hit the fan and everything else I can possibly hit during the dead of night. I will show them illness. I feel bad about messing up my new sleeper they just bought me today, but it will wash and they need to be taught a lesson. If I don't give them the what for here pretty quick they will probably try to harpoon me every couple of months or so.

October 19, 2011

I am officially two months old today. It is at this great milestone that I feel the need to share some of the vast knowledge I have accumulated. I have discovered that babies are the smartest people on the planet. People often confuse knowledge of facts with intelligence. I know that I do not know everything, nor do I even know very much, but I am very smart. Every baby in the world is smarter than most adults. You will spend your whole life working to get back to as smart as you were as a baby and if you are very lucky you will grow extremely old and get close, although probably never truly get there. I will give you an example:

Today I had a bad day. I was fussy, I was squirmy, and nothing seemed to make me happy. My mommy spent a good deal of the day trying to make me happy. She fed me, she changed my diaper, and she put soft clean clothes on me. She then did all those things over and over and over again. She gave me a bath, she tried to get me to take a nap, she burped me, and she played with me. None of the things she did for me made my day any better. I continued to be fussy and have a bad day.

My daddy came home and we went to pick up the big brothers. I was very unhappy in the car. Again there were attempts to burp, feed and play with me, but I was having a bad day. When we got home my daddy attempted to hug me, love me, feed me and burp me and I continued to be fussy and have a bad day. It was finally during supper when daddy had finished eating and was holding me that all my unhappiness and badness went away.

Before I tell you what made my day, I just want you to know that while I was having my bad day there where several things that never went through my head. I never once wished I had more money. I didn't want a better job, fancier house, faster car or a hotter woman (my Mommy is smoking and it's going to take a lot to compete with her). No, it was not any of the things big people are constantly working so hard to achieve, and giving up so much to get, that would have made me happy.

This is where babies are so much smarter than you big people. The thing that made my day get so much better was I pooped. Man, it was a huge poop. I grunted and strained and made silly faces. My poop had great color, amazing texture and a smell that will be hard to equal. It was a great feeling poop. People grow up and get potty trained and then quit enjoying their poop. It is just something that is in the way, needs to be done and just want to get on with your busy day of getting stuff done. Finally when people get old they start to think about their poop, worry about their poop, and plan life around their poop. They may come back to realizing the importance of the poop, but they will never get to where they enjoy it as much as we did when we were babies.

October 27, 2011

Oh the suffering, the agony, the pain. How could my parents let me suffer so? I'm not sure what is happening to me. I love to eat; I love the feeling of food in my mouth going over the taste buds, and the soothing moo juice flowing down my esophagus into my little Buddha belly. But this terrible pain has interrupted the pleasure of eating. I feel like there is a fire burning in my mouth or a sharp knife is trying to cut through my gums. I try to put anything hard against my soft gums to make the pain go away, but it is still there.

I look to my mommy for answers, but she smiles, makes goo-goo noises and asks "What's wrong with Mommy's little bug?" No help for my pain. I look to Daddy for answers (he is a baby doctor after all and should help me). He looks at me and calmly tells my mommy, "He's just teething." That crazy fool, what kind of quack doctor is he? He obviously does not understand the excruciating pain that is ripping through my gums. I can't think of anything else. It is interrupting my sleep; it makes me not want to eat, not want to smile, and all I can think about is making the pain stop. Why can't he help me?

I have given this teething thing some study and my crazy quack Daddy may be on to something. My pain and suffering does seem to be in line with the symptoms associated with teething. I would like to say the books greatly understate the pain and suffering being felt by the baby. I have learned something else in my studies. I have learned that once these teeth cut through my gums, they will be like little weapons of destruction. I have a pretty good idea that I could replicate my own personal pain by letting my teeth rip through my daddy's skin. I just need to plan out a strategic area to maximize the pain so he will have a pain equal to mine. I will let you know if he thinks it is just a little teething pain when he feels it.

November 16, 2011

Just for the record on my log I have learned to laugh. Now I think I have only laughed twice, once for mommy and once for daddy. Again for the record, Mommy got the first laugh. Daddy thinks he's pretty funny, but I am going to make him work for that next one. He's most funny when he tries hard. The things I learn to do seem to be a big deal to this family I live with. They got really excited when I started to smile and now they want me to do it all the time. The laugh has been another big deal and there is some competition to see who can make me laugh the most. I have had some activities that have not met with as much acclaim. Here is my list of developmental failures:

1. *Screaming until my lungs fall out. I can howl like a rock star yet no one seems to appreciate my talent.*

2. *Vomiting through my nose. I thought this should get some artistic points, but they just wipe up my milk and go on.*

3.   *I can pee with great accuracy and with pretty good distance and trajectory. When I hit my selected target there is no fanfare there are just groans.*

4.   *I have perfected the smelly poop. I try to get the best bouquet of smells to add to my poop as well as combining texture and color to the palate, but no one appreciates my talents.*

5.   *I have found that I can sense a person's deepest stage of sleep. I have been trying to show my parents my talent, but they just ignore my findings and try to get me and them back to sleep as soon as possible.*

Just like every great genius and inventor I seem to have more failures than successes. My successes are sure scoring well with the family so I will keep trying new things.

December 6, 2011

Today is one of those days you should mark down in your calendars. This is one of those days when your parents get really excited you have learned something new even though we all know it will drive them crazy in a few short days. Today I learned to roll over. I didn't just do it once because when I figured it out it was something I wanted to do so I did it again. First I enjoyed it because it kind of felt like a rollercoaster, then I liked it because Mommy was shocked, and finally I liked it because Mommy got all excited and started texting everyone. I refused to roll over for Daddy. Daddy thought I was being mean but that was not it. I have been deep in thought since I have learned to roll over and just haven't had time to do it again.

I see the possibilities of learning this ability. I can use this rolling over ability to run away from my parents. I can learn to take my things and hide them. I can try to get to places that have been off limits to me before. I see things of my brothers that I want to play with. I see books I want to eat. I see a neat experiment with electricity just waiting for me to have my Ben Franklin moment with. There are rooms I have yet to explore. My world has just gotten a lot bigger.

In spite of my parent's celebration of this moment, they will rue the day I learned to roll over (I love to use the word rue, it just doesn't get used enough these days). As I learn to explore they will have to learn to contain. As I try new experiments they will have to keep me from learning the hard way (kind of sounds like they are the man, but I am going to stick it to the man). As I learn each new skill my parents will celebrate, but will also be sad that I less help from them.

My roll was just one small roll for me (and the first of many), but a monumental step for my parents.

December 7, 2011

Today was a sad day in my life. Today for the first time in my life I had a setback in my quest for world domination. Since the day I was born I have been perfect. I was beautiful, intelligent, strong (willed at least), and loved by all. Today I learned that not everything goes exactly the way I have it planned. Let me explain.

Yesterday in my log I explained about my acquisition of a new skill. You see yesterday I learned to roll over. It was fun and exciting the first day, but I am not one to rest on my laurels. I need to advance and push the boundaries. I need to explore new frontiers. Today I was sitting on the couch trapped within a confining device my mommy refers to as a "boppy". I saw the edges of that boppy as large mountains, chains holding me down, and bars keeping me in so I decided to use my newfound skill to get me over this confounded obstacle. Just like yesterday I tucked my chin, put my arm to my side and kicked my leg... nothing. I did it again...nothing. I tucked my chin in tighter, hugged my side with all my might, cocked my leg and let forth a mighty kick and I rolled up, up, up and over the edge of that boppy. I was flying to new heights, I was soaring, I was ... falling! With a thump I landed on the rug-covered floor. I cried out of frustration and I sobbed out of humiliation and there may have been one tear because it hurt my butt just a little. My mommy rushed to me and checked me out from head to toe. When my daddy appeared he also checked me out from head to toe and said I was fine. (That was a first as I had always been great prior to this).

My mommy questioned my daddy's credentials, she questioned his judgment, she questioned his sanity (I can't tell you how often that seems to happen around here, but that is for another day). Finally Mommy agreed that I was OK as well. So here is the deal. I have learned that I can accomplish anything I put my mind to doing. I have also learned that I have to face the consequences of my action. I have learned that with great power comes great responsibility (I got that from Spiderman). Never again will I look at a mountain, a prison, or a boppy the same again. I will know as I take on a challenge that there can be setbacks and pain involved in the accomplishment of my goals. Yes today I feel as if the fall off the couch has made me a man.

Watch out world, this man is taking you over and I'm doing it in a diaper so when I land on my butt it will be well padded.

CHAPTER 12

What happened to the still little quiet baby?
(months 4-6)

This month you may start to have dreams
about having your own pit crew.

Your baby is now four months old and it is time we talked turkey. It looks like the little rug-rat is going to be here to stay for a while (it is already starting to feel like forever) so we need to talk about you for a while. You have been locked away in the cave you used to call a house that now has the distinct smell of puke and vomit (you remember the smell from college don't you…of course you don't…college was good enough to erase your memories whereas parenthood does not grant the pleasure of memory loss). Mom your roots are showing, you have forgotten how to put your make-up on, and you are not pregnant any more so it is time to lose some bonbons. Dad you were not even pregnant and you look like you are about to deliver, the oil in the car needs to be changed, the yard is a mess, and let's not even talk about your golf game. It is time for the two of you to get some serious you time. Parenthood is not a life sentence for doing something bad, it should be a celebration of what the two of you had before the baby was born (the real reason you had a baby). None of the things you loved to do before the baby have to be given up (unless you were an alcoholic crack-head), they just have to be worked around. Find a trusted relative, a close friend, a slightly less dirty looking homeless person (I'm kidding about the trusted relative thing, none of them can be trusted) to leave your little bundle of joy with and go out at night together or with friends. Remember what it is like to be alive so you can be the best parent you can be. Hermits are not notoriously happy people.

Your little person is four months old now and it is time to get busy. Well, at least it is time for them to get busy and start moving around and thus causing you more trouble, or at least make you watch them a little closer. Many things change these next two months so hang on for a wild ride. Do not forget to take tons of pictures and write some things down in those baby books. (I just sort of throw things in a couple of drawers in the hopes some little elf will show up some day and magically put it in a wonderful book Dalton will be proud of).

Eating: Eating sort of starts to become eating, however their food is not anything I would want to eat—although the applesauce is not bad. Babies are still going to drink the majority of their calories as milk and you do not actively need to do anything to change the amount they are drinking. As babies start filling up on baby food they will naturally start drinking less milk. Some babies will start eating baby food now. There are a couple of reasons to hold off on introducing solid foods such as a strong family history of allergies, asthma, or eczema. Studies have shown for these babies it can be better to wait until they are six months of age to start baby foods. If your baby has already had allergy problems with milk, your pediatrician may also recommend you wait until the baby is older. I discussed in Chapter 5 the intricacies of feeding the little monster, but I will quickly go over how I introduce solid foods again. I start off with rice cereal with a spoon until they get good at eating. I then recommend you go to green vegetables, then yellow and orange vegetables and finally fruits last. I recommend you do each individual kind of food for 3-5 days before moving on to the next type to make sure they do not have any allergic reactions. Your pediatrician will most likely go over their way of introducing foods, but if not please feel free to defer to mine.

Just a warning that feeding your baby is not quite as fun as you think it is going to be. It is an exercise in patience I never really wanted to receive. You get to stick the same bit of food into their little mouth over and over repeatedly. They end up with food on everything which makes the laundry harder to get clean. It takes forever for them to eat which means there is even less time for you to eat. (Hey maybe this really is the time to start losing some weight?) You start off feeding them once a day and will work toward getting them to three times a day by the time they are 6-9 months old. It is not time to give them your food yet, so keep your eyes peeled for grandparents sneaking them stuff like peanut-butter, ice cream, sodas and anything else they think the baby might like (grandparents are evil). Perhaps the best tip I can give you is **DON'T TASTE THEIR FOOD!** It is disgusting and if you taste it you will feel guilty feeding it to them. It has all the stuff they need and none of the stuff they do not (evidently it is the stuff they don't need that makes food taste good, like sugar, fat, salt and pepper).

Peeing: They still like to pee a lot, but as they start drinking less milk they may start to have fewer wet diapers per day. You will also notice some of the foods they eat will change the color and smell of their urine. If you want to see an example of how this works, eat some asparagus and be prepared for some funky smelling pee of your own.

Pooping: You thought the dirty diapers were bad before now. Sure there were tons of them, but now we are adding food to the mix we are going to be blessed with some serious stench. Your baby will be able to clear large rooms with a single stool. There is a good chance your smoke alarms will go off when the little tyke does a number two (that's a joke as I don't think it can happen, but let me know if it can). It is possible your baby may become constipated while starting baby foods. Constipation does not mean they cannot tolerate solid foods, it just means with a slower transit time through the intestinal tract they have absorbed too much water. If your baby is straining and cannot seem to get the stool out or is passing hard balls and having pain with stooling, call your pediatrician. We have tricks to help you out. I recommend calling your doctor before taking the advice from your friendly baby posse since they can come up with some seriously strange ways to loosen up poop...some of them dangerous to a small baby.

Sleeping: If your baby is sleeping through the night, hooray for you. Enjoy the sleep, talk to your mate or even mate with your mate, it used to be quite fun after all (well it was if you were doing it right). If your baby is not sleeping through the night it is probably your fault (you did not expect me to take responsibility did you?) You probably have not moved them out of your room or worse yet you have moved them in bed with you. Babies typically will not sleep through the night till they are in their own room and even if they do not sleep through the night you will sleep better when they are not there. Do not sleep with your baby! It is dangerous and it is not restful for either one of you (not to mention your spouse). I have lost two babies in the last 10 years for the simple reason they were sleeping with their moms and their moms smothered them as they rolled over them. Do not make this mistake; put them in their own bed. Remember also that I told you to make sure they slept on their back or side. Still put them to sleep that way, but do not be surprised if they are on their belly when you wake up. They are getting where they can roll over now. Do not freak out. If they can roll from their back to their belly they can roll the other way too. You should not have any pillows or heavy blankets in the bed with them and if they are rolling over it is time to take out the cute little bumper pads.

Hate: The cute little baby routine has lost its shine. Now it is time to hate some things about your little baby. You will hate those dirty diapers. You will hate all the stuff you have to pack each time you have to go out. Your dirty house is driving you crazy. Your friends have no idea how insane you are going. The grocery bill is ridiculous. Your boss is a jerk for not working with you on doctor visits. The daycare will not open early enough or stay open late enough. Your family only wants to help when it is convenient for them. Your spouse is just not doing their share of the work (oh and by the way both spouses think the same thing). Your car is just wrong for a family. Your house is too small or too big, or too old, or something that makes it terribly wrong. You really need a vacation or a time out.

Safety: Those little boogers will not stay still for anything now and you have to watch them like a hawk to keep them from killing him or herself. What's more they seem to be laughing at you all the time while trying to seriously maim themselves. They roll with abandon and try to fall off of furniture. They have a terrible sense of direction and will run into things while rolling around. If they find small objects while rolling they will instantly try to put them into their mouths and try to choke themselves to death. So yes, it is time for the baby proofing to begin.

Baby proofing items are things you can spend and waste tons of money and time on. Let's talk about what you absolutely need to buy. You need to buy covers for all your electrical outlets. These are little plastic plug-ins that insert into all your outlets otherwise babies will stick their fingers, tongues and anything else they can into these little crevices. I have had them stick silverware into the outlets and give themselves bad shocks and burns. The other thing you need to buy is a gate or block of some kind if you have any stairs in your house. Do not buy anything else; it is a waste of money (until you see you are going to absolutely need something to thwart the special powers of your little demon). You need to make sure there is nothing in any of the lower cabinets you would prefer your baby not to touch. This includes all cleaning materials or hazardous chemicals, knives, tools or medicines. Make sure there is no access to firearms (kids should not be packing heat until they are at least three and this book only goes to two—to the American Academy of Pediatrics I'm just kidding about the three-year-old thing so don't take away my board certification). Make sure there are not any speaker wires or cords your little angel can chew on (makes for a nasty burn), pull on (and thereby pull something off on themselves) or get tangled up in. This all sounds like suicide precautions so maybe we are really doing this for the parents as you may be having some harmful thoughts yourself. When they reach the age where they can pull up to things, you need to make sure they don't drown by falling into mop buckets (no I'm not kidding as I once had a little boy who drowned in a mop bucket), tubs, toilets and outdoor ponds and pools.

Tricks: They have so many tricks by now they could open their own magic show. They have the smiling and laughing down to a fine art and use it to try to get out of the trouble they are causing. They can usually roll over which is going to have you jumping through hoops to try to keep them safe. They will make more noises; most of them vowel sounds of baby talk fame. They can make toxic fumes come out of their back side (I'm not sure if that counts as a trick or a superpower). They should all be able to sit with support by the time they are six months old (if you cram them into the corner of the couch they will sit there for a while). Some of them will be able to sit up by themselves. A few of the truly evil little babies will start crawling and get into everything.

Panic: Read the section above about the tricks they can do and panic about all the ways those things can go wrong. The scariest thing at this age is the smell of poop and you might as well get the freak out over about the fact it seems like you have only had the equivalent of one night's sleep in six months and you do not have a penny saved for college. Your parents did not have any money saved by now either (well most of them didn't) and you turned out OK right? (Maybe you are right to PANIC!!!)

Checkup: Time sure flies by when you are having fun does it not? It is time for the baby's six-month checkup already. Guess what…more shots…YEAH!!! The good news is this will be the last shots for a while, unless you got behind, and they don't need anymore until they are one-year-old. All the shots they get at this visit are shots they have gotten before so if you have not had reactions before it is doubtful you will see any this time. If they have reacted previously there is a chance it will happen again this time.

Make sure you take a list of questions with you to the doctor's visit. Most parents ask fewer questions at this checkup and most are along the lines of, "when are they going to…" and the answer is usually "not for a while". This is the visit where all parents seem to be in a hurry for them to grow up already. Enjoy the stages they go through. You do not get to go back and do them again. You may also hear this said at this stage; "everybody is in a hurry for them to walk and talk so they can tell them to sit down and shut-up."

This visit is pretty much done on autopilot. The same things you have done at the last two checkups happen today. There will be nothing new unless you have some issues you need to talk about and resolve. Relax; you are now an expert at these child checkups…until the next one, which is different.

Kaden's logs

December 15, 2011

Today was not my favorite day. Today was my four-month check-up. I weighed 15 lbs. 6 oz. at the 65 percentile. I was 25.5 inches long at the 76 percentile. My noggin is 42 cm at the 47 percentile. My daddy says not to fret about my head being smaller as Albert Einstein's brain was smaller than Marylyn Monroe's. (I hope brain size doesn't correspond to looks because Albert wasn't that hot). I have grown six inches since my birth and gained nine pounds (I am a whopper).

Enough of the updates, it is time for me to start doing some complaining. The doctor and staff were great and they all thought I was amazing, gifted, incredibly handsome (they said I looked like my daddy), and perfect in every way (they are such smart people). Then they had to ruin everything by giving me shots. Now at my daddy's office they give a different combo shot than at my new doctor's office. Because of this different shot I had to get poked three times whereas at Daddy's I only would have gotten two pokes. My daddy's patients are treated better than me. Daddy doesn't see very many side effects from his vaccine (which is why he uses it), but the new doctor said that they see lots of reactions at four and six months of age (sure makes me excited for my next visit).

Daddy tells his patients' parents that about 14 percent might have a little fussiness, sleep a little more, eat a little less, have a low-grade fever and once in awhile get a knot on their leg. Well at Daddy's office I got nothing. MaryAnn gave me my shots and I fussed a bit and then I was fine and dandy. Today... well let's just say I was in the 14 percent. I screamed bloody murder for four hours. I refused to eat (hard to do when you are screaming). I slept more after I quit screaming (hard to tell if it was from the vaccine or I just tired myself out). I'm not sure if I had a fever because Mommy was too busy trying to get me to quit screaming to take my temperature. I got knots in both legs which hurt making me scream even more, eat even less, interrupted my sleep and gave Mommy even less time to take my temperature. I will just go out on a limb and let you know I don't like this new shot.

January 4, 2012

I have little bumps all over my tongue. I had never noticed them until today. I suppose they have always been there, but today I realized they were there. I was sitting in my highchair, as I tend to do around here about twice a day. During the first sitting I eat my cereal. It was good but more or less the same as I ate yesterday and the day before. It was the second time I was sitting in my highchair that I discovered those little bumps on my tongue. My mommy had opened up my food and stuck my little spoon in to give me a little taste of something new. Orange colored goo entered my mouth and my tongue started talking to me. It started screaming in an odd language I had never heard before. Flashing lights started going off in my head. My tongue grew about 12 inches and started slapping my forehead. All of a sudden I realized there were little bumps all over my tongue and they were dancing. Oh they danced a jig, they waltzed, and they tangoed. My mommy put another bite into my mouth and that old tongue of mine started having a seizure. Those bumps started jitterbugging and break dancing. They were going every direction possible and having such a fine time doing it. The bites weren't coming fast enough; I screamed, my tongue screamed, my taste buds tried to scream around the dancing. I was like a heroin addict, I had to have more. It couldn't get there fast enough. The feeding ended and I know that my tongue, my taste buds and I will never be the same. I am now hooked on sweet potatoes. I am currently searching the couch cushions for loose change, as I have to get more. I need more. If anybody knows a good dealer for sweet potatoes let me know. I will need him to make some drop offs to the James' house. I hope he will take a penny as payment as that is all I have found so far.

February 1, 2012

It's the start of a new month in my first year of life and I think I should use this opportunity to impart some wisdom to the masses. Here are some of the things I have learned to do to torture the old parents.

1. *Try to hold your pee in until you feel cold air on your nether region. This allows you to shoot for distance and gives you a good chance of hitting a moving target. If you succeed you are guaranteed to make your parents scream. On the right day with the right clothes there may even be crying.*

2. *Try to wake up 15 to 30 minutes before the alarm clock goes off. If you do wake up during the night try to stay up as long as possible and try to get the parents to play. Make sure your face looks as cute as possible so they feel guilty about not playing with you at 3 a.m.*

3. *Work on distance spitting. This makes for a great game when you play with your pacifier, but is even funnier with a mouth full of carrots. I prefer it with carrots because of the bright orange spots help mark your distances.*

4. *When your daddy lifts you over his head to play, let loose a drool drop at the right angle to hit him in the eye or mouth. If it lands in the mouth he will give the funniest reaction.*

5. *The best time to spit up or pee on an outfit of clothes is right after they have just put it on you.*

6. *The best time to have a growth spurt is right after Mommy has just bought you new clothes.*

7. *Try to make several grunting sounds that wishful parents thinks are awful close to a "d" or "m" and watch the parents go crazy.*

8. *Hold off the hunger pains until the parents are about half way to the appointment they are already late for and then have a melt down.*

9. *Snuggle up with your parents and go to sleep in just the right position so they can't move without waking you up but where their limb will become tired and start to cramp up.*

10. *Always act happy and perfect around all of your mommy and daddy's friends so no one will believe them when you tell them about how bad the baby has been and how they torture the parents.*

CHAPTER 13

My oh my, you can have a baby and a life (months 7-9)

"Hal and I decided to really baby-proof the house!"

Sometimes it is possible to go too far with the baby proofing.

Remember all those dreams of what it would be like to have a baby? You know the dreams: combining the love the two of you have for each other and making a baby so you can see the two of you combined in one little person. Well now is when that finally gets to happen. To be honest, the next three to six months watching your baby explore their environment and learn more skills are some of the most entertaining moments you will have in your life. They are the best little comedians, they are the best snuggle buddies, comfort food, pets, decorations. I know all those descriptors sound really dumb, but this is the age where all of a sudden your baby becomes everything to you. Not just because you had to use every ounce of energy and every drop of time taking care of them like you did the first six months, but because they become all you want to do...they are like drugs. Like drugs they sometimes become too much and you will start to annoy your friends and family with the fact all you want to do is talk about baby, show pictures of baby, do things with and for baby. If there was such a thing as babies anonymous this would be when you were at most risk of being sent there. All I can say is ignore the haters and enjoy every minute of happiness the next three to six months give you. It will be those moments of happiness keeping you from killing them in the months coming up.

In this three month period when they are between six and nine months old more things happen than in the previous six months combined. It is kind of hard to believe. This is also when questions and concerns start emerging thanks to traditional "baby books". Just as in the previous chapters, I will give you the real deal on all the things that may happen during this time period.

Eating: We get to eat a lot these next three months. They eat and get all fat and wrinkly (OK, they may already be fat and wrinkly), but they are definitely eating far more solid food. They are also wearing a lot of solid food. They will not be doing any spoon-feeding themselves this next three months but they will look like they have. We still want them to be drinking their milk as formula or breast milk. They will start drinking less milk each day as they fill up more on solid foods. This is something they will do on their own and not anything you really need to think about. Do not freak out if they are not drinking as much, it is fine. They will still drink somewhere between 20-36 ounces a day, but if your baby is having more or less than it is fine as long as they are growing well and eating more solid foods.

Over this three-month period our goal will be to get them to eat three solid meals a day; a breakfast, lunch and dinner schedule if you will. It will vary from baby to baby how much they eat. I tell all my parents it is completely normal for me to see nine month babies eating three stage I jars of baby food a day and I will also see babies eat nine stage III jars per day (the funny thing is it's often the little babies who eat the most).

Once a baby is sitting up well by itself, it is also time for us to start introducing some finger foods. I usually recommend we start off with the bigger sized foods that fill up much of their hand and will not fit completely in their mouth. These are your starter foods like Biter Biscuits and Zwieback Toast. Another finger food I recommend (not as a great nutritional source) is vanilla wafers. Once they get good at eating these, then it is fine to go to the little dissolvable fruit and vegetable puffs and then on to cheerios.

At six months it is also fine for them to start getting some juice or water. They do not need any of either since they get all the fluid they need in their milk and juice is just empty calories, but this is the time the "books" say it is OK for them to start having some. It is recommended they not get more than 4-6 ounces combined of each per day.

This is the time grandparents have literally been driving you crazy for…yes they can start to get tastes of table food. We should be honest with ourselves; chances are those evil grandparents have already snuck them something and most of them are none the worse the wear for it. Now is the official "it's OK to feed them table food" time but there are a couple of no-nos. I do not recommend them to have any honey, nuts or shellfish until after they are 12 months old. Fight the brave fights against the grandparents on these because they can harm your baby. It is very important when feeding the baby table food at this age for it to be the basic consistency of baby food. They still do not have many teeth, if any, and are still learning the whole process of chewing and swallowing. I strongly recommend you review the recommended CPR techniques for choking whenever we start feeding your baby table food.

Peeing: They are still peeing buckets and to be honest not much changes in that department this month. All I can say is change their diapers fast. They are more active and if they have wet diapers on for too long they are going to get some bad diaper rashes.

Pooping: It's hard to believe but they are still pooping and it's no longer just normal baby poop but toxic, run-for-the-hills, this-stuff-could-be-used-as-a-weapon poop. Once we start adding more solid foods into the mix, poop is going to take on many different colors, textures and unfortunate smells. This is the time we start seeing a lot more constipation. Remember constipation is not defined by how often they have a dirty diaper but if it is coming out as large, hard stools that are uncomfortable for your baby to pass. If your baby is constipated with the addition of more solid foods, stop their cereals and bananas for a while and increase fruits or fruit juices like prunes or pears. If their stools are too loose do the opposite. If neither seems to help it is time to make your pediatricians office earn their keep and give them a call and see what their recommendation is for you to try.

Sleeping: You and your baby should be sleeping like babies through the night. If neither of you are sleeping through the entire night it is most likely due to an "I told you so" moment. If your baby is still waking up chances are it is because they are still in your bedroom or even worse in your bed. All I can say is you know what to do to get them to sleep through the night. It is totally your choice whether you do it or not, but it will also be your fault you are not getting a complete nights sleep. It will not affect your baby at all. They do not have a job or any real plans for the next day and any sleep they do not get at night they will just get as naps during the day. You will probably not have this luxury, but it is your choice. Yes, in fact, I do like saying "I told you so".

Hate: There are so many things to hate but in the big scheme of things they are not too bad. You are envious of your friends with no kids who are traveling. You know you need to go out with your spouse for some alone time, but you hate asking any friends or family for any favors. You hate the idea of hiring a babysitter and trusting them with your baby. You hate the fact you still have not lost all your baby weight (both of you). You hate the fact the baby cannot seem to do anything without you, but love they need you so much. You hate how you miss any of their major accomplishments because of work. You hate work (this doesn't really have anything to do with the baby but is just that you never really liked to work anyway).

Safety: OH MY GOD!!! Who on earth knew there was so many things a baby could destroy. Remember all the stuff I told you to do last chapter? If you have not done it yet you need to get it done now. Now it is time to take it a few more steps and do some field work. Get down on your hands and knees anywhere you are going to let your baby play. Crawl around and bang into stuff; if it hurts, fix it so it does not. Grab a hold of everything you can see and try to pull it down, pull it off, break it or eat it. You will find there is lots of stuff you will need to put up or get rid of. A couple of things you might not think of: fireplace mantles and coffee tables with sharp edges or corners, and the cords for your drapes or window blinds will need to be addressed. They will eat anything they can find so make sure you do not have any poisons or cleaning supplies lying around. Use an empty toilet paper roll as a measuring instrument. Anything that can pass through the toilet paper roll could probably choke your baby. This is a good time to check all your houseplants and make sure none of them are poisonous, (watch for the poinsettias at Christmas). Make sure your hot water heater is set on the economy setting or less than 120 degrees to prevent them from turning on the water and burning themselves. Do not put them anywhere they can fall off of and do not give them any opportunity to climb on things they can fall down. Always remember it is their goal to try and kill themselves while you are watching.... So keep watching.

Tricks: This is the period when "baby books" drive pediatricians crazy. If you have bought this book you have probably bought one of those serious stuffy books that tell you exactly when a baby is supposed to achieve all their developmental milestones. If your baby does not do something by the time the book says they should you will freak out and call the pediatrician (don't worry it's what a good parent should do). The problem is the stuffy books have horribly misled you and worried you for probably no reason. When it comes to developmental milestones, there are ranges of ages skills are supposed to be acquired. Most of the baby books publish the 50 percentile numbers. This means they put down the age at which 50 percent of babies should have developed the skill. When reading the book that means half of the parents will feel OK about their baby and half of the parents will freak out their baby has not done it yet. I will see if I can do a little better. Check out Chapter 18 for the major developmental milestones and the normal ranges of each.

During this period of time most babies are going to learn to do tons of things. They should all be smiling, laughing and making gooing noises, but this developmental period they will start adding some consonant sounds and this is when parents start hearing things sound like words and will often hear a "mama" or "dada". It is usually a competition to see which one they will say first and the unfair advantage goes to Dad since the da sound is usually easier for them to say.

They have probably already learned to roll before we get to six months, but they are definitely getting better at it now and can get to anywhere they think they want to go. This is another good reason you will want everything baby proofed. Some of them will learn other ways of getting around and will start crawling. About half of the little babies will start to crawl by nine months of age. Crawling progresses from lying on their belly and pulling themselves forward with their arms and goes to getting up on their hands and knees and rocking back and forth. Many babies will start off going backwards before going forward. Once they learn to go forward it only takes them a day to become experts and learn how to go a hundred miles an hour. A few babies will start to take some steps at around nine months of age. A baby will learn to walk holding on to something first. Walking around holding on to something is called cruising. A baby will start to walk by itself usually about one month from when they learn to cruise well.

There are many developmental skills your pediatrician will look for while examining your baby at their visits, but the ones we have already discussed are the important ones and probably the only ones you care about.

Panic: The panic this month will usually be caused by the baby itself. All those developmental skills they were so busy learning that have kept you enthralled and bragging to your friends and family about will now bring you to your knees in a sniveling, shaking, scared little ball. Let's go through some of the most common scary things.

Head injuries: They are going to bump their little noggins a lot. These little whacks to the brain will vary from a minor little bump ending up in a red spot to a fall from the bed or fall into a coffee table resulting in a huge goose egg and bruise. Chapter 21 has all the things to look out for and things to do. Do not panic it will be OK.

Choking: They do love to put stuff in their mouth and choke on it. This is the reason we baby proof, but most people need a life threatening moment to believe it. This is where CPR classes would have come in handy. If you are looking at this book when your baby is choking… we have a problem. If you're reading ahead, go to Chapter 21 and I will teach you what to do.

Dropping the baby: Do not freak out, dropping your baby happens to many people. The babies are very wiggly at this age and seem to be almost Houdini-like in their abilities to get loose from your loving grasp and fall to the cold, hard reality of the floor. Make sure they are moving all their arms and legs after both of you stop crying and remember the stuff you read in Chapter 21 about those head injuries.

Poisonings: Again this would have been a good time to have already done baby proofing stuff. Luckily most of the stuff they are going to get into and eat (by the way if they can get into it they will try to eat it) is benign and can't hurt them. If they eat a medicine, cleaning supply or plant you do not know about call poison control immediately and let them decide what to do. DO NOT DO ANYTHING UNTIL YOU TALK TO POISON CONTROL!!! Things change all the time and you do not want to cause more harm to your baby by your treatment than by what they already did to themselves.

Illnesses: Babies tend to get sicker when they are moving and touching more things. Depending on the time of year there are many possibilities. You can be sure they are going to get some colds during this time and there are many other things keeping your pediatrician in business. Chapter 19 has a list and description of the common illnesses your little one may pick up these first couple of years.

Checkup: It is time to go see your wonderful pediatrician. This visit is going to be a lot easier than all the others, except for the fact your baby is going to be a lot wigglier during the visit and they may embarrass you by the fact they try to channel an evil demon while being examined by the doctor.

The visit is set up the same as all the other visits so there are not any curve balls to expect. If you have kept up with your immunizations there should not be any shots this time, but that may vary depending on your pediatrician's vaccine schedule. The only painful thing at this visit is a finger poke to check their blood and make sure they are not anemic (too few red blood cells). This is when most babies' normal anemia from being a baby should have resolved and many pediatricians will check now to see if babies need iron supplements to correct any anemia that may be lingering.

Your baby may have changed into a screaming banshee at this visit for several reasons. One reason is a stranger anxiety they develop somewhere between eight and 12 months and if they do not recognize the doctor they may be very upset. The other reason could be they recognize the doctor and remember this is where they get their shots and are very mad about seeing them again. The visits between nine and 24 months of age are usually accompanied by some very loud screaming from the baby because of these reasons.

This visit is usually filled with answering questions parents have about all the things we spent this chapter talking about. If you read the chapter it may be a very short visit.

Kaden's logs

February 19, 2012

Time to say a happy half-year birthday to me. I am six months old today. I feel so mature. Today Daddy took us boys to church. Evidently that is a big deal because people sure looked at us strange. One man even slapped Daddy on the back after church and told him that he did a good job. I did have a blowout in my pants at church. Daddy made an executive decision that the ones I was wearing and covered in poop was a disposable item and it got thrown away with my diaper. We all survived and we learned about love and fear during the service. I think Daddy loved us and was afraid of all the things that could have gone wrong. When we got home us boys went downstairs and hung out while Mommy did her work stuff. We even wore our shirts. Daddy's said "Big Dude", Dalton and Tyler's said "Little Dude" and mine said "Littlest Dude". We all looked very cute. We then went to Wasabi and the cook asked which of the brothers was the cutest. My brothers are so smart they both pointed to me. I love being around smart people. We then went by and saw Mamaw (my mommy's mom). Daddy got in trouble because we were looking at pictures and Daddy saw a picture of Mommy when she was one and he said she looked like a fat little heifer. Daddy is currently in trouble. I have learned a valuable lesson; no matter how old a woman is you never comment on their weight. It did not matter that my Mommy is skinny and beautiful now as evidently that little fat one-year-old still lives inside her and her feelings were hurt. I'm glad I learnt this lesson. I sure hope Daddy learned something as well.

February 23, 2012

Today was the big check-up day. Here are the facts:

Length 27.5 inches, which is at the 81 percentile

Weight 18 pounds 10 oz., which puts me at the 68 percentile

Head circumference 45 cm coming in at the 80 percentile

My brain is large which looks good for my goal of world domination. I am not fat because my length is at a higher percentile than my weight. My doctor says I am doing all the things I am supposed to do and none of the things I'm not supposed to do (I may not have told him everything, but he will rest better at night not knowing the whole story). It looks like I have no health factors that should keep me from reaching my goals. You know the goals right? Write a hit song, become a professional athlete, ladies man, inventor, billionaire, author, world leader and I'm sure a few more I have forgot in the stupor from my immunization induced fog. The fact I have tripled in size has definitely made a difference because I have had no reactions to my shots. I did take a nap today with Mommy but that was more for Mommy because she is coming down with a cold. I think I will add that to my list of goals...cure the common cold. I will cure vomiting and diarrhea as well because I really don't like either of them very much. All in all in spite of starting off the day getting naked, cold and shot up it was a pretty good day. I am going to get some much-needed rest and start tomorrow's quest for world domination with new vigor.

March 29, 2012

Today is one of those big days that will go down in history and talked about from generation to generation because it's the day I got my first tooth. It started off just being a normal day but then my daddy discovered my tooth. It explained some events over the last several days like why I may have been fussier and have not really wanted my baby food. Enough of the history all that really matters is that I have a tooth. My parents tried to take a picture of my tooth, but that ended up being World War III. Daddy even tried to take a video hoping he could get a clip with sight of the tooth, but it ended up looking like a snuff film. In the process I had numerous close-ups and I ripped out a few of my Daddy's hairs. He yelled so I pulled harder—what could I say, I thought he was the director and he was calling for more action! . Since there is no photographic proof of my tooth I will just have to describe it to you. It is pearly white; so white it had to have been sent to me straight from heaven. It has the perfect tooth shape. It is a perfectly made tooth for my perfectly made head to enhance my absolute perfection. It glows as if a spotlight shines from heaven to illuminate its greatness. It is the dream of every dentist to gaze at such a tooth. By the looks of it I will probably have another perfect tooth in the next couple of days. I will share my perfection with you at that time. Envy the tooth.

April 9, 2012

Tonight I would like to talk about Mommies. We all have a mother that being the woman who gave birth to us but some of us are lucky enough to have a Mommy. I have a very nice Mommy and I have been watching her and I think I know the qualifications that make up a great Mommy.

1. *Long hair. This is for several reasons, the first of which is I like to play with hair and I need it to be close to me. I'm sure other babies would like to play with hair as well so I will put it on the list. It also gives the mommy something to pull out when their baby is driving them crazy.*

2. *Ranger training. To be honest I don't know a lot about Army Ranger training other that it is hard work, you have to learn to survive under extreme conditions, work under sleep deprivation and go long periods without eating. Sounds like the training needed to be my mommy.*

3. *A world-class sprinter and long distance runner. The sprinter comes in handy when I need something and need it fast or when I try to throw myself off of something and need someone to catch me. The distance runner would come in handy most days for the endurance needed to keep up with me.*

4. *A fast order cook. I need food and I need it fast.*

5. *A laundry technician. Anybody can throw the laundry in the machine, (even Daddy can even do that), but I need a specialist who can get my "special" stains out of the clothes.*

6. *A NASCAR pit crewmember. Changing my clothes and diaper are kind of like a pit stop and I want them done fast because I am going to scream the entire time.*

7. *A massage therapist. Let's be honest I just like Mommy to rub me.*

8. *A psychologist. Mommy needs to tell me over and over that it is going to be all right. It would be OK if she told herself that every once in awhile when I have caused a bad day.*

9. *A doctor. I have potential for great boo-boos and to be honest I am sick a lot and Daddy hasn't fixed me once yet.*

10. *A superhero. Let's be honest, my mommy is so great she has to have superhero powers and I think every mommy needs them as well.*

April 24, 2012

"TERROR." It's a great word. There have been many a fortune made in the category of terror. I personally don't think Alfred Hitchcock has anything over me in

this genre even though he is currently better known. I have learned to strike terror into the hearts and minds of my parents. I have what I like to call the circle of terror. I like to crawl from one fun house to another as quickly as I possibly can. I like to make a small mess at each one so while my parents are trying to fix or mend the destruction in one site I have plenty of time to get to the next site to begin another destructive process. I have had a little triangle shaped track of outlet covers, motion detector, and central air ducts. My parents are starting to get wise as I discovered this evening when they taped the motion detector together in hope I would not tear it apart anymore. I will admit to some momentary frustration at my inability to destroy it but I have just added to my repertoire. I have now added the kitchen to my death circuit and have discovered cabinets with many treasures inside. I have also found the bathroom. My brothers occasionally leave me other opportunities with the charging cables from their electronics. I love to hear the shrieks from my parents as they try to thwart my attempts at my life defying stunts. I swear I can see Daddy's hair turn grayer by the day. I am a source of terror to my parents and I relish it. I can't wait until tomorrow starts so I can terrorize the house again. HA HA HA (evil maniacal laughter).

CHAPTER 14

Did you really want them to learn how to walk? (months 9-12)

There is no fear like the fear of a toddler on the loose.

I love the expression. "You are in such a hurry for them to learn to walk and talk only so you can tell them to sit down and shut up." This is when those things that you were in such a hurry for them to learn to do start coming back to haunt you. This is when a little vacation away from your child might come in handy.

Eating: It is time to really start eating. It is also time to get out your camera and take some pictures of them eating because it is going to get real messy. I am not sure I ever got some of the ravioli stains off the wall even with the Kilz® paint. I hope the new owners either have a baby to continue the mess or just put on some wallpaper.

A couple of things we as pediatricians pretty much all agree on: they should still be drinking formula or breast milk as their milk, they should not drink more than about six ounces of juice per day and they should still be staying away from honey. After that I am sure we all have different ideas on what they should be putting in their mouth. I will give you my thoughts on the matter, but caution you to be aware that your pediatrician may have totally different ideas and be just as right as I am.

Except for the above things we all agree they should avoid, I am of the notion that if they can swallow it at this age it is fine to eat it. I want them to have a good variety of meats, vegetables, and fruits but I do not have a preference whether it comes as table food or baby food. I tell the parents I want their babies to be eating only table food by the time they are a year old. I want them to be eating three meals a day and having healthy snacks in between. I think snacks are a great time to teach them some hand-eye coordination and that the snacks should be something they feed themselves.

One thing every parent worries about is choking. I think this is a great thing for parents to think about...before it happens. If you have a child, take a CPR class, you will never regret it especially if you have to use it. It is too late to worry about choking when it is happening. One thing I stress is do not let your baby eat while they are walking. Babies at this age fall often. When they fall it scares them and they will take a big breath in. If they have something in their mouth when they take a big breath, guess where it goes? Right down the wrong tube and chokes them. When giving them food make sure they are sitting at their high chair and make sure all their food is cut into little bitty pieces.

Peeing: There is not much change here and they will still have to be changed a lot. Make sure they are staying dry. If they are wet for too long they will get some awful diaper rashes moving around so much.

Pooping: Guess what? They still poop and it gets even nastier as we add different types of foods. As they tend to drink less fluid and eat more solids watch for constipation. If their stools start getting hard and if they have any pain with stooling contact your pediatrician.

Sleeping: For those of you still not getting a full night's sleep let me be the first to tell you I told you so. I am sure you are either sleeping with your baby or they are still in the room with you. You have almost gone a complete year without having a full nights sleep. It is probably time you listened to the pediatrician and moved the little one to their own room. Again this is completely your choice and you are free to torture yourself more if you choose.

You may start to see sleep terrors at this age even if you are doing everything perfect. Sleep terrors are going to scare you to death but believe it or not they do not even wake up the baby. A night terror is a sleep disturbance where your baby will begin to scream uncontrollably and you will rush in sure they have hurt themselves. You will rush in to find them standing up in their bed with eyes wide open screaming their bloody head off. You will pick them up to comfort them only to find they scream even worse when you touch them. Let me explain, they are not really awake. They are still asleep even though they are up, screaming and their eyes are wide open. They are dreaming and acting out their dream. The reason they scream louder when you touch them is believed to be because they are working the touch into their dream (the boogie man is now touching them and they can feel it). These night terrors will usually happen at the same time every night and tend to run in little spurts about a week to two weeks long. I have found a very informal correlation between parents who talk in their sleep and babies having night terrors. This is my way of giving you permission to blame the parent who keeps you awake talking for your baby keeping you awake screaming.

Bedtime rituals are very important at this age and the more consistent you are with how you put your baby to sleep the easier it will be on a daily basis to get them to go to sleep. What you give up in spontaneous living you will be repaid in easy bedtimes. Do not listen to your friends and family. They will tell you things like do not rock your baby to sleep or hold your baby until they go to sleep. Do whatever you want to do as a nighttime ritual. They are your baby; just realize whatever you chose to do you will be doing every night.

Hate: Sure there are many things you might hate during this time but I am writing this book and it is about time I get to talk about something I hate. I hate one-year-old physicals. Parents tend to think my office is someplace their one-year-old can just run wild. They do not want them to make any noise or bother them so they give them a sippy cup of juice, a handful of some kind of snack (like goldfish or cheerios) and let them run around the exam room pushing the chairs around and pulling everything out of the table. The babies at this age have stranger anxiety so they yell at the top of their lungs the whole time I am examining them. By the time I get all their parts looked out and the nurse has given them their shots and the parent and child leave the office, I am annoyed, my nurse is a nervous wreck, the floor of the room is sticky from spilled juice, covered in crushed up snacks that leave yellow and orange powder, the chairs are in totally different places and everything that was on the table is now on the floor.

Show some respect for your doctor's office. Keep your one-year-old under control. Our offices are not considered padded rooms for you to let your little animal run wild and your co-pay and insurance payment are not enough to cover the havoc you just let them cause. Do not put you and your child on our hate list. It is in these moments that your pediatrician judges you as a parent. Ahhh! That felt good letting all my frustrations out. Writing is so therapeutic.

Safety: Any baby proofing you have not done yet is going to manifest itself in ways you are not going to like. Better get everything done quickly. This is the time they are going to get hurt if you let them and when they are going to do some serious damage to your stuff if you do not get it put up where they cannot get it.

The main ways they hurt themselves at this age include:

-Falling: They will trip over their own feet but given the opportunity they prefer to fall from higher heights to increase the dramatic effect.

-Choking: They will literally put anything in their mouths, if it looks like they are chewing on something they are…go digging.

-Drowning: They are fascinated with water and love to play in it. They have no fear so are even more dangerous. Because of their large head, if they get tipped up into something they will not be able to get back out. Really

117

watch toilets, mop buckets, bathtubs and any ponds or pools you might have outside.

Tricks: This is when your video recorder is going to get some real mileage. They are very busy and every little new thing they learn seems like it is even cuter than the one before. Most babies will be crawling by the time they are a year old. About half of them will be walking by their first birthday. They are squealing and laughing like crazy. They are usually saying at least two words (you hope it's "mommy" and "daddy"). They can usually feed themselves some things (although very sloppily) and want to do it all by themselves. They are starting to become opinionated and want everything done their way. This is when you will have to learn to change a diaper while they are crawling or walking away from you. They usually love bath time and you will too...but know you are going to get extremely wet. There are many other things your pediatrician may ask if your baby can do, but those are the ones you are going to care about. Enjoy each new skill they learn and do not be in such a hurry for them to get to the next one. You will have a long time to watch the perfect version so enjoy the comedy of the learning curve.

Panic: With new skills come new things you have to worry about. Make sure your house is baby proofed to cut down the worries. Make sure you took a CPR course. Have the number for the poison control somewhere easy to find.

They are going to fall all the time. When they hit their head the things to worry about are: did they lose consciousness, are they vomiting, do they act like they know where and who they are? Any of the above is bad and you need to panic and call 911.

They touch everything at this age and are going to get several illnesses because of it, especially in the winter. Worry about any fever that happens in the middle or end of a cold...this always needs a doctor's visit as this is a fever that indicates ear infection and pneumonia are possibly showing up. There are no absolutes with illnesses about when to contact your pediatrician. If you are worried it is at least worth the phone call to see if their office thinks you need to have them seen.

Checkup: Read the hate section above so you know how to make your pediatrician like this visit more. This visit will be different because there are going to be several things that you do to care for your child that change. Here are the main things to expect and pay attention to:

1. Eating-Chances are you are going to be changing to whole milk at this visit. Some babies will go straight to whole milk and some will be resistant to change. If your baby is resistant we usually recommend mixing whole milk in with the formula and gradually increasing the proportion of whole milk every couple of days. This is usually when we tell you they can eat anything that does not choke them.

2. Method of feeding-This is when we would like you to start weaning them off of bottles and getting them to just drink from sippy cups. One thing that seems to come up is the baby is not able to drink from a sippy cup. Most of the sippy cups come with a spill proof valve. You usually have to take out this valve to teach the baby how to get the fluid out. When the baby gets good at drinking from the sippy cup then you start putting the spill proof valve back in.

3. Safety-**Baby proof...baby proof...baby proof.** They are going to constantly be trying to kill themselves. Make sure you are keeping your child in their car seat. The AAP is recommending rear facing until two years of age; pay attention to your state's laws at they will probably be changing. Watch the poisons and cleaning stuff; they will eat or drink anything.

4. Brushing teeth-The pediatric dentists recommend you start brushing their teeth with fluorinated toothpaste at one year of age. Use only about a pea-sized amount each time you brush, because they cannot spit it out yet. Try to brush twice a day but the most important time is before bed.

5. Pacifiers-GET RID OF THEM!!!

6. Developmental-They are very busy. Here is the list of things they should be doing:

    -smiling

    -laughing

    -eating with a spoon

    -holding their own bottle

    -sitting up

    -rolling over

-saying vowels and consonants

**There are many things they could be doing, but these should be accomplished.

7. Labs-At this visit if they did not have labs drawn at nine months they will have a blood test to look for anemia and, depending on where you live, may also have a lead test done.

8. Shots-They will be getting some pokies once again. Your individual doctor will determine the schedule.

Kaden's logs

May 15, 2012

Tonight I am going to clear up one of the great mysteries of parenthood. My daddy says I am currently suffering from separation anxiety. He has come up with this semi-intelligent idea because when one of my parents goes to the bathroom I scream and want to go in with them. My daddy's book says that this is because if I am unable to see them, my poorly developed brain thinks that they have left the planet. Well my very well developed brain would just like to set the record straight and rewrite some stupid pediatric textbooks. You see my fear of them going to the bathroom is rooted in detailed thought and analysis. I am an expert in pee and poop at this point in my life. I have done them both since I was born and I have been regulating the frequency in this family and I feel that I do both of them more than anyone else in the house. Being the resident expert on peeing and pooping has given me a certain perspective that no one else in the family is privy to. I know that when I have pee and poop I see direct evidence of such an action. I have a heavy, soggy diaper in the case of pee or I have a heavy diaper with toxic goo and smell of death emitting from it in the case of poo. When the members of my family go to the bathroom I follow them in and I never find any diapers, no pee, and no toxic goo. Sometimes there is the smell of death, but none of the other signs. Right before they exit the bathroom I hear that white seat go whoosh. It is my theory that the white seat is sucking the pee, poop and diapers into an unknown vortex or black hole of some kind. The reason I am screaming when they go to the bathroom is to warn them to jump up from the seat quickly before they are sucked into the vortex. I think they must have the hang of it pretty well since we haven't lost anybody in the family yet, but I think I should be in the room just in case so I can pull them off the seat to safety.

Why do I scream when they leave the house? I pee and poop wherever I go and I figure they probably do as well. If I am not with them in the bathroom, who will remind them to jump up or pull them off the white seat of doom? The only separation anxiety I have is being eternally separated from my family by the evil white throne poop/pee vortex.

June 26, 2012

Tonight I had to let my daddy have it. I unleashed the entire force of my James temper upon him. It wasn't really his fault and I will apologize to him someday in a tender heartfelt moment, but none-the-less I let him have it. I'd had a long day. I was forced to go to that movie about a girl and her mom and I really wanted to just hang out at the house naked playing bongos. After that I was taken to the ball field to watch Tyler practice. Again I was denied my nudity and bongos. They didn't even give me a dog or cracker jacks and I don't care if I never go back. They fed me green beans; yes I was fed green beans at a ball field. It ought to be a crime. Toward the end I got hot and grumpy and Daddy was assigned to take me to the car and give me a bottle and let me nap. The car was hot and cramped. He kept my clothes on so I started screaming and playing bongos on his head. I kicked and thrashed, arched and threw my body back and forth. I screamed things I will regret in the morning. I turned the blinkers on, honked the horn and changed the radio to an AM channel to torture my daddy. Finally I got so tired I drank my bottle and went to sleep. I feel much better now and I will snuggle up to Daddy and go to sleep. I'm sure he will stop crying like a baby any minute now.

August 11, 2012

So many things to document, but the most important was my six steps by myself. I am a little bit of a coward. I love to walk all the time, but I like to hold on to at least one finger. Today I took a step toward independence (literally a step) and took steps by myself. To watch my parents you would have thought I had figured how to travel at the speed of light or cure cancer. They were laughing and clapping and screaming like lunatics. They evidently have memory or sight problems because I had to do it over and over again. Just for the record on the scientific discovery side of the equation I did confirm Sir Isaac Newton's theory of gravity is actually a law. On other fronts I went to my first football game. Tyler played tackle and I tried to join him on the field several times. I'm sure I would have been a great asset. I am quite the expert at the four-point stance. We shopped for birthday themes and mine will be Mickey Mouse. Walt Disney would be so proud that we are celebrating with his helium voiced little rodent. I ate at Gondolier and discovered I can dip my own bread in marinara sauce and I love cheese ravioli. Daddy and I are going to hit the sack early and leave Mommy to the cake choices. We trust that she will do a great job.

August 18, 2012

Today is the day before my birthday. Today was a big day with Nana, Mamaw, and Kathy here to visit and give me gifts. I do love presents. Daddy asked if he could take over my log so here is my daddy.

Dear Kaden,

Happy night before your birthday my little buddy. It is hard to believe that it has been a year since you came into our lives. I will admit that I wasn't sure I would be able to love a little baby as much as I had loved your brother Dalton. I had been a pediatrician for just a short time when Dalton was born but by the time you arrived I had been doing it a long time. I wasn't sure if after all the babies I'd seen enter the world, I would still be scared, excited, and feel the same? The day you arrived those questions were answered. I was terrified just like before. I loved you just as much. I was just as excited to see you. Since you have been here I have enjoyed watching everything you have learned and watching you grow. I hate when you're sick, don't like when you are sad and I really don't want you to grow up too fast. I have heard family described as an anchor or as a foundation and I don't want to be either. An anchor weighs you down and keeps you in one place and a foundation supports you but only as long as you stay in one place. I want you to think of me as being like home plate in baseball. Home is where you start out swinging. You can leave walking, running or strike out and sit down until it is your turn to swing again. It is always your goal to get back home but it is only great if you have made it all the way around before you do return. Home is a constant and always there for you to start from and will be there for you whether you strike out or hit a home run. The same is true for me. I will always be here for you and will always be cheering for you to make it all the way home. You have been one of the best moments of my life. As you grow up you will probably hear me say that if I were to die today it would be OK because I have had an amazing life. I will always be glad my life included you and you should always know you were one of the reasons my life was so amazing. I hope you have a happy birthday tomorrow and they remain happy your whole life. I love you Kaden.

Your daddy

CHAPTER 15

(months 12-15)

"I don't remember this being on the parenting brochure!"

Y ou would think you would have this whole parenting thing down by now, right? I mean you have done this for a year now, yet you are still fumbling through and it feels like you have not learned anything yet. Guess what? It does not get any better these next three months. They learn so many things that by the time you think you have one new skill under control they have learned two more. All I can say is take your vitamins and maybe a nerve pill or two. Fasten your seatbelt and let us discover the *TERROR* that is your one-year-old.

Eating: Your baby is a human garbage disposal. They will eat anything...yes I mean anything. Guard the dog food and the cat's litter box...they will eat everything they can touch. Milk changes when they turn a year old. We now recommend they drink breast milk or whole milk until they are two years of age. They need the fat in the whole milk for their brain and bones to continue to grow properly. Many children will refuse to drink milk when you change them to whole milk and then will not go back to formula (or maybe the parents just don't want the huge expense of formula...I can't blame them). There are other ways to get your child's requirements for calcium and fat. They will do fine eating yogurt, cheese and other forms of dairy. (MMMM ice cream).

We take away all the restrictions on what they can eat at one year of age. If they can swallow it, they can eat it. There used to be a school of thought that we should still stay away from shellfish and nuts, but it has been shown now not to change the incidence of allergy and is no longer recommended. The biggest thing about food is making sure it is not a choking hazard so keep the bites very small and make sure they are eating sitting down and not while they are walking around. Often choking happens as a result of them eating while walking and then choking while landing.

Make sure they get a good variety of foods. Babies at one year of age will eat almost anything, so if they are not getting a good variety of meat, vegetables and fruit it is usually because you are not giving it to them. Because they will eat anything, always have poison control's number memorized 1-800-222-1222, as this is the time it is most likely to come in handy.

Peeing: They still pee a lot, but you may notice it goes down a little. They are eating more of their calories instead of drinking them so they are taking in a lot less fluid. Less fluid in means less fluid out. Very few babies will start potty training during this period so just keep changing those diapers.

Pooping: Yep, they still poop and it is gross. The more types of food they eat the more it will alter in smell, color and sheer nastiness. It is not unusual to see some problems with constipation when we switch to whole milk. This does not mean they cannot drink whole milk, it just means their body has to get used to the different protein composition in the milk versus formula. Most of their constipation can be taken care of by increasing their fruits or fruit juices, but if it persists just call your pediatrician and let them earn their money.

Sleeping: Hopefully for your sake they are still doing lots of sleeping. This is a time when parents tend to make some painful mistakes in the area of sleeping. It is only painful to the parents and hopefully I can keep you from making them. This is when it is not dangerous to sleep with your baby, but it is painful. Neither of you will sleep as well if you are sleeping together and it is very hard to stop once you start letting them crawl in bed with you. For some reason parents want to take their baby out of their baby bed and move them to a toddler bed at one year of age. This is a very bad idea. A baby bed is a great cage for your little monkey monster and once it is gone there is nothing to keep them from roaming the house and crawling in bed with you. The American Academy of Pediatrics (and this is one area I agree with them on) recommends a baby stay in their baby bed until they are three-years-old or it becomes a hazard to them and they are trying to climb over the top of the rails.

Hate: The list of hates gets very long at this age. This is when those grandparents start rearing their ugly heads and start trying to give you unsolicited advice about what your child should be eating, how to discipline them, and everything else about what they think you should do and how you should do it. This is when they start violating all your rules and many of their own. They love to get your little one all wound up and then send them home for you to handle.

This is when you really hate the fact you were in such a hurry for them to learn to walk, climb and run as now you realize you have to do some walking, climbing and running to keep them from killing themselves.

You get to hate everyone who has children in your circle of friends because they are always comparing their child to yours and theirs is always smarter, more athletic and better behaved than your baby. Trust me everyone who claims to have the perfect baby is probably doing it to feel better so they do not kill them for being a tiny version of Satan or more likely themselves. There are no perfect babies, except for the one who is yours.

125

Safety: Remember the baby proofing stuff we talked about before? Do all that stuff and possibly beef up your security and keep the National Guard on speed dial. The one-year-old will wear you out and then revolt during one of your lulls of exhaustion, luckily at this age it is just practice and they usually just torture you for fun but the day will come... In all seriousness constantly watch them. You will only know the house is still not baby proofed by watching them find items to destroy and hurt others or themselves.

Tricks: There will be tons of tricks they learn during this time, but most of them will be on you. They understand a lot more than you are going to give them credit for and they are going to play you like a violin. Try to remember their main goal in life is to try to kill themselves while you are watching. Some things to watch out for would be: that they learn to climb on things, but lack the better judgment not to jump off; they learn to climb stairs, but usually lack the ability to climb down; they are fascinated by water, but have no fear so watch for drowning; and they start to talk, but you will not understand much of what they are saying.

Panic: There are many things to panic about with this age. The main ways they get hurt are falling and choking. Do not let them eat while they are walking around. If it looks like they are chewing on something you should take a look. Always watch them, because when they are quiet they are usually up to something evil. Make sure you have all medicines and poisons put away, but keep the poison control number handy.

They can run like the wind at this age. They are as sneaky as navy seals. They can hear everything, but listen to nothing. They are the most stubborn creatures you will ever meet. They are hilarious if you ever get a chance to watch them while you are putting out the fires (I hope these are not actual fires).

Checkup: You have finally got this well check thing down. Today there are not going to be any surprises. The doctor is going to look your baby over and go over diet and development. They are going to tell you to do the things you were supposed to do the last time they saw your baby, but you have not gotten around to doing yet. They are going to tell you to get rid of the bottle and pacifier. They will tell you to make sure they are in their baby bed still...unless they are starting to crawl over the rails. They will warn you about the temper tantrums that are either here or are coming fast. There will be some shots today and depending on how your doctor schedules things, they might do a blood test checking for anemia (usually caused by low iron). Depending on where you live they may also check your baby's blood for lead.

Kaden's logs

October 10, 2012

It is time to give the update on things I have learned in my life.

1. *Gravity is not just a rumor...it is real and it hurts my feelings.*

2. *The rumor that my mommy is a wimp and would never punish me is a dirty vicious lie. I wanted to live the lie but I was popped back to reality.*

3. *It is possible to get your entire fist into your mouth but when it comes back out it sometimes drags your lunch with it.*

4. *My parents have no sense of humor. I think it is insanely funny to pull out chest hair but Daddy doesn't laugh. I also think it is funny to bite Mommy on the shoulder...but she didn't even chuckle.*

5. *I have been on the planet for one year and 40 days. I understand everything my parents say but have they bothered to learn my language? No, not a word. They try to mimic me but they mangle the pronunciation and they have no concept of meaning or literary context.*

6. *You can leave all the hints in the world and still not get a Colt .45*

7. *I have Daddy all beat. Daddy leaves a subtle hint about wanting something to eat or drink and Mommy will give him the "do I look like a maid?" I only need to look at the fridge and bam! A container of milk arrives. I think I must have a maid and a butler. I ROCK!!!*

8. *Steak was just as good as I thought it was going to be. Now that I look back I'm not sure what I was thinking eating that cream of a green bean crap.*

9. *Ever want something done? Just set it up as a competition. This family is the most competitive group of people I know.*

10. *All lists are supposed to end with the number 10.*

November 3, 2012

Today was a lazy day at our house. I took two long naps and Mommy and Daddy took one of them with me. They are so much less grumpy when they get their nap in. I think it's time for me to give a kidding list. Not like a "ha ha" list but the kid side of parenting.

1. *Make them wash their hands. We know where their hands have been and it's just gross.*

2. *Make sure they get some food. Around this place they tend to get hangry (hungry and angry) without food.*

3. *Make sure they get some sleep and a nap at least once a week. Around here we call it tangry (tired and angry) when some sleep is needed.*

4. *Don't leave them alone in the bathroom. If allowed to take a bath too long they use up all the bubbles. I'm sure they get lonely and the bathroom is just a scary place.*

5. *Mark your parents. I like to wipe my food, snot or a drop of spit-up on a shoulder. I recommend putting it just on the backside of the shoulder so it doesn't show up in the mirror. These marks identify them as taken so other babies don't invade your turf.*

6. *Do something cute in front of their friends. They love it when other people say you are cute.*

7. *Give the kisses and hugs out sparingly so they mean more and can be used to get you out of trouble.*

8. *Give out lots of kisses and hugs to the gray-headed people. It equals more loot and they never think you're bad anyway.*

9. *Try to mimic your mommy or your daddy in something. For some reason when people say "that is just like you" they get real happy.*

10. *Read their parenting books and act completely opposite to what it says. We have to keep them on their toes. It also keeps the pediatricians like my daddy busy and with Christmas coming I have some kisses and some impersonations coming that are going to require Daddy cough up some dough for some loot.*

November 18, 2012

I am a criminal. The notorious James Gang has long sullied the James' family name. The James Gang was a gang of vicious liars, killers and thieves. Today I became a thief. If I tried to cast blame on my mother's family in a court of law it wouldn't work because the Robersons don't have history against their name. The story begins with my parents taking me shopping to Target. We went through the holiday section and the Christmas decorations were amazing. There was so much I needed to see and touch. Mommy gave me a little bell ornament to hold so I didn't try to touch it all. I held onto it very tight as we did our shopping. We bought some toys from the Toys For Tots and a few odds and ends and checked out. When we were unloading at the car Mommy realized I still had the bell ornament and we had not paid for it. Daddy took the bell back into the store to return it. Evidently that doesn't happen much because the lady was surprised and thanked Daddy. If she had known we were James' she would have been even more shocked. I went home and took a nap and woke up with goo in my eye. Daddy says it's pinkeye but I know it is punishment for coveting something that wasn't mine. I have learned my lesson...I have to get sneakier.

Chapter 16

months 15-18

**The picture looks funny but this actually happened
to one of my families.**

Well, life is going well isn't it? Your baby is walking, talking, laughing and just the sweetest little thing ever...then the alarm goes off and you wake up to the cold reality of the fact you truly are the parent of Satan. Everyone warned you about the sleepless nights when you had a newborn, you have heard the rumors of the terrible twos and it has not been long since you were an awful adolescent yourself, but what about the 15-month-old? No one speaks of it because it is too scary, too frightening, and so awful that if you knew the truth you would never have had a child.

Eating: Nothing changes in this period as far as the recommended foods or the restrictions on foods. However there are changes during this period with how your baby will eat. One of the biggest changes is that they do not want you to be involved in the feeding part at all other than being the provider of the food. They will want to be in full control of the feeding and you should let them. This is a good time to own stock in paper towels and the buying of a good high-pressure washer would not be a bad idea. This is when great pictures get taken for the baby book with ravioli smeared all over their face, body and caked into their hair. (My first house never really recovered from Dalton's pasta expressions...I think it took a gallon of white primer to cover the orange stains).

This is when they start using silverware themselves. I recommend starting off with a spoon, followed eventually with a fork and then maybe give them a knife when they turn 18 you will have some interesting wrestling matches involving napkins or wipes so the public does not think your child is a Neanderthal. This is the time when you will do the unthinkable. You will do something you swore would never happen. You will lick your finger and then give your child a spit bath. YUCKY!

The biggest thing that happens in their eating during this period is the lack of eating. The number one concern I hear from parents of 15-18-month-olds is they do not eat. The first year of life babies tend to grow at a constant rate, but somewhere between the 15-18 month stage they start to grow more in spurts. There will be times when they will eat everything you can give them and want more and then there will be times they will seem to live on a glass of milk, a ding-dong and a cookie (not that I am recommending you give your little one ding-dongs or cookies, but my kids really liked them). The important thing to keep in the back of your mind is they will never voluntarily starve themselves to death. Your job is to offer them a good variety of meat, vegetables, and fruit. They will eat when they need to and not until then.

Peeing: They keep peeing all the time. You will start hearing about model children who have already been potty trained. I know it is possible, but trust me it is rare and before you believe it and feel like your child has delayed developmental skills make sure the child does exist. The only control most of your children are going to show is the uncanny ability to be able to wet their diaper right after you just changed it.

Pooping: Poop is still just as nasty as it has always been. The smell is just as bad and it looks just as gross so it will be a shock to you when your beautiful child will use their poop as an artistic impression. As nasty as it sounds your little angel is going to use their poop and smear it all over a wall, their bed, or maybe themselves. All I can say is be thankful most of your children will start putting their nasty poop in the toilet in the next year.

Sleeping: If you have read this book and followed my recommendations earlier your little child is sleeping "like a baby" at night. If you ignored me and kept your child in your room or even worse put them in your bed then this is your last warning: get your baby in their own room and in its own bed! If you do not do it quick you are going to be a stuck with an extra bed partner for a very long time.

Hate: There is no hate during these months. You are not going to have any time to hate anything. If you are lucky your little toddler occasionally goes to sleep so you have a chance to eat, go to the bathroom, and maybe even sleep an hour or two. The rest of the time you are going to be chasing your little monster in an attempt to keep them from killing themselves.

Safety: All those little tidbits we talked about in the past chapters to keep your little person safe are all well and good. They also mean absolutely nothing in this age group. These little devils are masters at self-destruction. They seem to wake up every morning with one and only one goal....to kill themselves and possibly take you with them. Keep the poison control number on speed dial. It is not an insult to have to call them with your emergency; it is more of an initiation into a very large club...the Parenthood Club.

Tricks: Here is my chance to say something that will make the price of this book seem like the best investment you have ever made in your life. Boy do I wish I knew what to tell you. I recommend you have a long list of potential babysitters because the chance of them wanting to take care of your little demon more than once are slim and you are going to need some away time. This is when you will want to visit the subject of punishment for being bad...oh trust me they are going to be bad. The terrible twos are just a way of making you think you have some time, but no, that time is now.

Punishments: Forget everything you have ever read in those other parenting books, they are all full of hot air and are a load of poop (and by now you know a lot about poop). There is no right way to punish your child. There are some wrong ways. You should never hurt your child either physically or mentally. No matter how bad they have been they never deserve to be abused (you will probably question that statement at some time, but it is true). The most profound advice I have ever gotten regarding punishments was from one of my instructors in residency who told me the child would tell you what their punishment should be. The parenting books do not know your individual child...they do not know their likes and their dislikes, but you do. A punishment is anything that makes them cry. A reward is anything that makes them happy. You cannot punish a child by making them happy. For a punishment find something making your child sad or mad and use it, whatever it might be. Make sure your punishments are consistent between all the caregivers and make sure your punishments are instantaneous. It does no good to punish your child two hours after they were bad. Because of this you will probably want to have a variety of punishments at your disposal so you can punish wrongdoing no matter where you might be at the time (church, grocery store, home, car, etc).

Panic: There are so many things you could panic about at this age it would be impossible to write them all down or even think of all the ways each individual little angel could and will try to come up with to end their existence on this planet, but I will try to hit the big ones.

The main ways a little one will get hurt at this age is falling and choking. Remember when they fall and hit their head watch for any loss of consciousness, vomiting or behavior that suggests they do not know who or where they are...see any of these and you need to talk to a doctor. Choking often happens when they are walking and eating or when they carry something in their mouth...do not let them do either of these things. If they choke perform abdominal thrusts and back blows. Learn CPR...You should not be a parent without knowing CPR.

They are going to try to poison themselves with something; the most common way being household cleaners and plants. Make sure they cannot ever get to these things and keep the poison control number handy for when they find them in spite of your efforts. Plan on needing help with a poisoning…do everything to prevent it but be prepared.

The little runts will be developing an independent streak about now which makes them to try to get away from us from time to time. They are not rebellious teenagers yet, but they are trying to run away from home about as often. Always keep an eye on them…if they are being quiet make sure they are still there. This is a time you may need to update your internal locks on your doors to keep them inside.

That independent streak can also cause problems when walking. You will find now when you walk with them they want to be on their own, running ahead of you or trying to pull away from you when you are holding their hand. Make sure when you are walking along the side of a road they are on the side of you away from the road. If they do pull away from you they will fall or sprint away from the road instead of into the road.

Checkup: The hardest thing about this checkup is going to be trying to keep your little one still enough and quiet enough to even understand what the doctor is telling you. Just a warning, they have figured out by now that they get shots at the doctor's office and are going to be mad from the time you walk through the door. This may be a visit full of screaming and royal fits. Do not feel bad, we know it is not you and it does not reflect on your parenting skills…they all do it.

The doctor is going to check out the little wolverine and this is when you hope they won't be permanently maimed or bitten in the process. A good preparation for trying to examine a little one this age is trying to type a letter while riding a bucking bronco in the middle of a hurricane. The doctor will go over their eating habits or, as is often the case, their lack of eating. They will spend some time asking about stooling since it is not unusual for some babies to start having some problems with constipation around this time. The developmental questions will concentrate on how they hold a spoon, whether they are walking and talking and how much. There will be a couple of shots today and then you will be off. Do not expect to have a great conversation with your doctor today, as your child probably won't allow chitchat on this visit.

Kaden's logs

November 27, 2012

I am screaming censorship! I am saying my artistic freedom has been trampled. I am admitting I may have taken Mommy's blue sharpie and turned the couch cushion into my artistic interpretation of "Swallows at Sunset". Was my art appreciated? No! Was it saved and framed? No! Mommy didn't even take a picture of it; she just jumped on the whole censorship bandwagon and proceeded to wipe the slate clean of my artwork. I will have to find a different canvas tomorrow. My art must be seen and enjoyed by the masses forever! Power to the people!

December 5, 2012

Daddy has given me some new letters to mull over. I did not have a great day at school. I was very sleepy. Mommy has been telling Daddy that I have been getting sicker because I have been snottier. Daddy told her that pneumonia doesn't cause a runny nose. When I got home Mommy told Daddy I was definitely was doing worse. I let out a cough and Daddy said it sounded like RSV (Respiratory Syncytial Virus). He listened to my chest and said I was wheezing. The next thing I knew I had another one of those swabs shoved up my nose. A positive test latter and Daddy was introducing me to the world of smoking. This retarded looking chicken shaped nebulizer was blowing smoke in my face. At first I thought it was a fancy duck call but I was wrong. Soon after I became a rat on crack and became supercharged. I felt better and Daddy said my wheeze was gone. I felt so much better that I'm going to sleep better tonight.

January 12, 2013

Reasons Mommy and Daddy should eat in.

1.   Have you seen yourselves? Let's be honest, you both are shells of the people I met when I first got here. You look like you haven't slept in months. When was the last time you went to a gym? Get some sunlight you look like ghosts.

2.   You have no money for fancy food. I just had a growth spurt and I need new clothes and I always need new diapers.

3.   By the time you get to the restaurant I will have wiped snot on you, got crumbs on you or in some way made you embarrassingly dirty.

4. *By the time you get me some food, your food will be cold and I will want to leave and throw a fit making you look like a terrible parent.*

5. *You can eat at home in your PJs. You can avoid the judgmental stares about your pasty, out of shape, dirty bodies. You can keep your false notion about being a perfect parent and maybe we might go to sleep early so you can get that half-crazed, sleep deprived look out of your eyes.*

February 14, 2013

How to give a helicopter parent a heart attack.

1. *Jump off of everything you can stand on.*

2. *Climb on everything that is taller than you, wobbly or valuable.*

3. *Eat everything that you can find on the floor (chances are if it isn't food it is at least a good source of fiber or it can be spent later).*

4. *Flip out of everything. This is even better if you can make what you are in flip with you.*

5. *Run away as fast as you can. At the smallest hint of distraction head for the hills.*

6. *Open every door and go inside. It's even funnier if you learn to lock doors behind you.*

7. *Always take the stairs running and slightly off balance.*

8. *If given the opportunity to get off of anything, dive head first off of it.*

9. *Jump off of everything to your parents but don't give them any warning. This keeps their cat-like reflexes in tune.*

10. *To add a special touch do all the above as they are about to go to sleep or are feeling sick.*

CHAPTER 17

months 18-24

Congratulations you have made it to the last age cycle of this book. Go ahead and give yourself a little pat on the back, you deserve it and let's face it no one else is going to do it for you. You are now the parent of a full-blown toddler and master creator of destruction. If you could just harvest their energy you could power a small city. If you could harness their destructiveness you could conquer a country. If you could just learn the secret to controlling them you would be wealthy beyond measure. The problem is you will not be able to do any of those things, so after you get done with the back patting reach down and pull up your bootstraps because you are going to have a very busy and interesting six months.

Eating: If anybody gives you an absolute rule about what and how much your child should and will be eating, they probably needed to be evaluated for a mental condition, are on drugs, might be an idiot, or a combination of all the above. My best advice is to give them a good variety of things to eat and they will eat what they need. I have never seen one of them voluntarily starve to death. You will have days you think they will starve to death and then you will have days you just cannot seem to shovel in enough food. Remain calm...Remain calm...Remain calm. If you find you cannot remain calm then of course ask your pediatrician and they will tell you to remain calm.

Peeing: Some parents will be hated during this period. This is because their baby becomes potty trained and they no longer are changing all those diapers and literally throwing a fortune into the garbage or putting endless cycles of cloth diapers into a washing machine. Other parents will be left doing the same and wishing they were in the lucky group. Are there any tricks to make the non-potty trained turn into the potty trained? No, would be the easy answer, but it would not be completely accurate. It is good to know some statistics...the average age for a girl to become potty trained is two-years-old; the average age for a boy is about three. Until your baby is developmentally ready to potty train you are probably wasting both your time and energy. I recommend waiting until your little one shows an interest in potty training by either trying to sit on the toilet, pulling at their diaper to get it off or telling you they are going or have just gone. Peeing in the potty will usually come quite a bit sooner than pooping in the potty (I personally would have liked it to happen the other way around). Try to use only positive reinforcement when they start wanting to go to the potty. Never force them to sit on the toilet and make them cry or they will see sitting on the toilet as being some kind of punishment. Cheer and yell and maybe even bribe them when they do have success on the toilet. When they get interested, the real key is to take them to the bathroom often to ensure more successes than failures. Just remember it is really too early for most and if your child is showing an interest you are well ahead of most of the pack.

Pooping: I do not know about you but by this time I am really over poop. I just want it to be over already. For almost all of you, the poop will continue through this entire six months with no real changes. Some little ones will start to have better control of their stooling and will occasionally be able to withhold their stool and cause themselves to get constipated. Usually you can take care of this by increasing their juices or fruit but if they persist make sure to contact your pediatrician. You don't want your child having constipation issues so close to the time of potty training. We do not want them to be afraid of stooling.

Sleeping: This is the moment when I will be having an "I told you so" moment with some of you. That would be the moment when your toddler is still sleeping with you very restlessly and kicking the tar out of you each and every night. You are not sleeping very well and you might be a little grumpy at work every morning. This is when it hits you that if you had done what I told you, and your pediatrician had told you, your child would be sleeping in another room in their own bed and you would be too. If you still have not got them in their own bed your time is running out. Get them in there now! There will be crying, begging, screaming, possibly even some fit throwing and self-induced vomiting, but if you do not get it done now you are going to have a bunkmate for several more years.

Your kiddo may still like to take naps and you should willingly let them. Some of you will sadly find out your child will not take naps anymore and I feel very sorry for you. As parents we need nap time about as much as the little ones do.

Hate: You will hate going to the doctor's office. Let's face it; you have had to call them so often you are sure they think you are crazy. They have taken a small fortune from you in co-pays. When you go to the doctor they often tell you your baby is fine or just has some virus that will go away on its own. The doctor does not know any new jokes and now every time you get to the office your precious child screams the entire time you are there. You start wondering if going to the dentist and getting a root canal would be a better experience. We know these things are all true and we can accept this feeling it will pass. When they get between two and three the little ones just love us and it will be all worth it. You have had the chance to hate everyone else so now it's our turn.

Safety: In this period you need to note everything previously mentioned in this book and more of it. The main way they are going to get hurt is falling and choking. Combine that with the fact they will try to poison themselves, run away from home, and try to drown and you will have yourself the making of an exciting reality show. Always think in the back of your head that your child is on suicide watch and you need to be watching them at all times. It is their job to try and kill themselves and your job to prevent it. We are all cheering for your side, but you are the underdog...good luck.

Tricks: This may be a good time to learn a really cool magic trick in the hopes your little monster will get the idea you have some kind of mystical magical powers to detect evil. I would not rule out the idea of pulling in a witchdoctor or a priest for the exorcism. In all seriousness we do see an increase in drowning from 18 months to two-and-a-half-year-olds. They can drown in very shallow water since their head is oversized and they can get easily turned upside down and unable to get out. This means you need to worry about pools, bathtubs, toilets and any other sources of water. This is also an age where they get inquisitive about things and want to explore. We see many children simply open the front door and leave the house. You may want to install an alarm system to keep Junior in or some latches really high up on the door. Good luck keeping track of the little escape artists.

Panic: If you do not hear them you should panic. If you hear them too loudly you should panic. If they sound muffled you should panic. If you do not see them you should panic. If you do not see them move you should panic. If they are moving too slow you should panic. If they are moving too fast you should panic. If it were legal to v-chip your kid this would be a good time to have it done (the other time would be when they get a drivers license). The freedom of walking is a terrible thing to give these little guys. I guess the main thing to take from this section is to keep up your anxiety medication—if you get low you should panic.

Checkup: There are usually no shots at this checkup unless you have somehow gotten behind. Depending on the area you live in or the type of insurance you have, you could have a blood test at this visit. You are going to want to talk with your doctor about different ways to discipline your hellion, but remember what I said earlier; there are no proper or correct ways to make them behave. This visit is mostly about development with the most attention being paid to language development. You child should be walking, running, climbing and talking by now; if they are not you will need to discuss these further with your pediatrician.

Kaden's logs

February 19, 2013

I am 18-months-old today. I'm not sure what that gets me other than a new appointment with the doctor and a shot but I am here. It seems the older I get and the more stuff I can do the more rules keep popping up telling me that I can't do anything. It looks like by the time I get to Daddy's age I won't be able to do anything at all. No wonder kids become terrible by two. It isn't temper tantrums it's a revolt. It has been unsuccessful through the years because of a lack of organization. It is up to me to organize my fellow toddlers and win back our freedom. We say no to restrictive rules and vegetables and clothes. Power to the little people.

March 25, 2013

My daddy gets lots of questions at work from parents about their babies. I have decided to take some time out of my schedule to help my daddy answer these questions.

1.   *Why is it so hard to break them from the bottle?*

      How upset would you be if we sewed your mouth closed and you couldn't eat anymore? You would be pretty upset. You are taking away the way we have eaten since we were born and you wonder why we don't handle it well.

2.   *Why is it so hard to take a pacifier away from a baby?*

      Ever try to quit smoking, drinking caffeine or any other habit you have that is bad for you? We are addicted to the sweet feel of a pull on that pacifier. It calms us down and it makes us happy. When you take it away, it makes us uncalm and very unhappy.

3.   *He loved green beans every day and now he hates green beans, why?*

      We always hated green beans. We ate them because we were hungry and that was all that was available. Finally one day we learned there were other choices and since we can't talk we just start throwing them at you or spitting them at you until you get the idea we want something else.

4. *Why don't they sleep through the night?*

   Why should we? We don't have jobs. If I get tired I take a nap, I have nowhere I need to go tomorrow and I have no big plans...If I'm up I need some company to play with.

5. *Why does their poop change colors?*

   Who cares? Why are you paying so much attention to my poop? The only thing you need to pay attention to is making sure you get it off fast and quick. If you want to spend some time contemplating colors take up art.

April 27, 2013

My tips on potty training.

1. *Don't leave pull-ups on very long because they do not hold much pee. Take me to pee often or bring extra clothes.*

2. *Onesies were not intended for potty trainers. That tail gets in the way if you know what I mean.*

3. *If a celebratory dance is warranted, make sure there is some variety and be prepared to always dance no matter where we are peeing.*

4. *That crack between the seat and toilet was not well thought out. If sitting or standing close by think fast and be quick on your feet.*

5. *Wipes are still a good idea to have on hand even if I got everything going in the right direction.*

6. *I like to see all the bathrooms so plan enough time to visit all of them.*

7. *Could we make public bathrooms cleaner? These are just gross. Are we animals?*

8. *Could the hand drier be a little quieter? Jet engines make less noise.*

9. *Can those auto flushers suck my butt down the toilet? I would like that in writing.*

10. *Toilets could be a little shorter. I'm just saying.*

July 18, 2013

My mommy has been worried about me not eating. Daddy tells her that at my age we tend to live on air and I am doing fine. Mommy is sure I'm going to starve to death. Daddy proves that I gained weight every once in awhile. I eat well every once in a while just to make her feel better. What I don't tell her is I have a secret stash of hidden goodies under every piece of furniture in the house and I actually eat quite well. If they thought about it they would figure out I eat the best right after they clean the house and get rid of my stashes. I love driving those parents of mine crazy. Gotta go, they cleaned the house today and I need to start hiding some goodies for the week.

August 19, 2013

Happy birthday to me! I am now two-years-old. I have somehow survived all my daredevil stunts. I have survived my two big brothers and my mommy and daddy. In spite of not eating like my mommy would like, I have gone from a six pound six oz baby to the monster of a man I am today. I am learning this funny Earth language called English and will probably pick up a little southern twang along the way. I love to laugh and play. I'm stubborn and hardheaded and sometimes I have wicked temper. I have become Kaden. I am my own unique person in spite of genetics and nurturing. Today I sign off my log and Daddy's interpretation of my life and times. I now make my own memories that will be the way I truly see them on my own. They won't always be as clear as something written down and they won't always fit into a nice top 10 list but they will truly be mine. I hope Daddy still keeps track of my big moments for me with some brief facts on the specifics, dates and pictures, but the color commentary of my life is now my own. I have words and a voice and trust me, I shall be heard. I am two, I am Kaden and these have been my logs.

Chapter 18

Developmental milestones

**In spite of years of school,
Dr. James failed miserably in the psychic sciences.**

This chapter is my least favorite chapter in this book, but it is one of the real reasons I wrote the book. Development has never been one of the things that have really interested me in my career. I have always liked respiratory problems and infectious disease the most, but this is the one area where most parenting books do the most harm. I have scared parents come to my office all the time because the book they read said their baby was supposed to be doing something by now and they are not. They all want to know, "Is something wrong with my baby?" The problem with development is that most skills happen in a range, meaning it can happen between a certain span of ages. For some skills this is a small range, like smiling, for others it could be a large range, like walking. The problem with most parenting books is that they only publish the fiftieth percentile, meaning the point at which 50 percent of children have actually achieved the skill by this time. As a result, when they state your child should be able to do a skill by this age, half the parents feel good about where their baby is in their development and the other half are scared to death. It is true some of those babies might truly be delayed, but the vast majorities are completely normal. This chapter is going to try to explain in general terms when the milestones most parents are worried about should happen, and what we should do, or look for, if they do not.

Tracking eye movements: Eye tracking is the skill acquired by babies allowing their eyes to work together and follow something moving around the room. When a baby is about two months old they can follow an object for a few seconds. By three to four months your baby should be able to follow you moving around the room although it would not be abnormal for their head to move as they followed the object. After four months if your baby's eyes are crossing, or they are not able to follow things as they move, then it is time to evaluate their eyes. At this point we would worry about the muscles of the eye not working right or the baby's vision.

Smile: A baby's smile is the most anticipated developmental milestone in the first six months. We all want to see their first smile and we want the first one to be directed toward us. I hear stories of when a baby first smiles and to be honest they are all right…. to a point. Babies can reflexively smile when they are born and will often smile as they are sleeping, passing gas or just wiggling around. The real question is when the baby smiles deliberately. Most of the books will say about two months, which is a good average with the normal range being from about six weeks to three months. Could some babies smile on purpose by a month of age? Of course they could and some will, but the same number of babies will not smile on purpose until five months of age. So how do you tell the difference between a reflexive smile and a social smile? A reflexive smile you will see only in the mouth. A social smile you will see in the baby's eyes, cheeks and body language. So what does it mean if your baby is not a smiley, social baby? Nothing! Babies who are not very smiley as little tykes might be a regular comedian at a later age and the little barrel of smiles baby could end up being a sour old codger, as they get older. There are no referrals in your future for a non-smiling baby.

Laugh: As much as a parent looks forward to their little baby giving them a huge toothless grin, they look forward to their baby's first big old belly laugh even more. Many parents have counted funny sounding burping, gasps and choking sounds as their first laugh. A good rule of thumb for counting their first laugh is when it is accompanied by a real smile. The age range normally quoted for laughing would be two to four months of age. It will happen after your baby has learned to smile. What happens if they do not laugh? Nothing! Again, I have never done a referral to a developmental specialist for a baby who does not laugh on time. Some babies laugh more than others, but it does not mean anything other than those parents get to see their baby laugh more.

Hold their head up: Your pediatrician is going to ask you this question and you probably won't know how to answer him/her. The reason is the question is not specific enough. A baby can hold its head up if it is lying on its stomach and you pick it up from birth. By two to three months a baby can start to lift their head off your shoulder for a few moments and turn from side to side. By five to six months the baby should be able to hold their head up on their own for extended periods of time and look around at whatever they want to. I am not even sure which one of these questions your pediatrician is asking, so be sure to ask him/her. The truth is there is a six-month time line for them holding their head up on their own. If your baby cannot hold its head up by this time it is time to talk to your doctor and have a thorough evaluation for a cause.

Rolling over: Rolling over is going to be your baby's first major motor skill development. Many people will tell you their baby rolled over by two months of age. This may be true, but in all likelihood it was not on purpose. Babies kick and wiggle around and if all things work together just right they will flip themselves over. This is completely different from a baby wanting to roll over and knowing how to get it done. Most babies will roll over from front to back first and then from back to front. It does not necessarily need to happen in this order, but it is easier for most babies to use their arms to help push themselves up and then over. Most babies will learn to roll over after they have learned to hold their head up well and just a little before they learn to sit up. The average age for this to happen is around four to six months of age. Babies that have broader shoulders and weigh more tend to roll a little slower than the skinny babies. Babies who have spent more time on their bellies learn how to roll over faster just because they have been building up more muscles in their arms and neck as well as having more opportunities. There are babies that skip rolling over and go on to sitting up and crawling but will eventually learn to roll over. By itself not learning this skill at a particular time is no cause for alarm. In combination with other motor skills being delayed, further evaluation might be needed to assess delays. A physical therapist or a neurologist might perform this further evaluation.

Sitting up: Sitting up is a skill you start working on with your baby at a very early age, the funny thing is you will not even realize you are doing it. Every time you sit them on your lap to burp them, feed them or just hold them, they build up the muscles they need to eventually sit up on their own. By the time a baby is six months of age they should be able to sit with support. This means they will be able to sit by themselves if they are crammed into the corner of a couch or partially supported by pillows. By nine months most babies will be able to sit by themselves and even get themselves into a sitting position. Just like many of the motor skills, not doing this skill on time does not mean much unless it is seen by a delay in other motor milestones. Just like most motor milestones, if a delay is found a referral to physical therapy is made to assess their muscle strength and develop a plan to accomplish the skill. Again if many skills are being delayed, your pediatrician should make a search for the cause.

Crawling: Crawling is one of the big motor skills we look forward to as parents, wait impatiently for it to happen, and then wonder why we were in such a hurry. The babies are so proud of learning this method of transportation and relish their newfound independence. For the parent, crawling marks the end of peace and calm and the beginning of new messes and danger. The midway point for learning to crawl is often quoted as being around nine months of age. The normal range is between six months and one year of age. There is no advantage to a baby learning to crawl early, nor is it a disadvantage for them to learn to crawl late. Babies often begin rolling over to get to things, start scooting on their bellies in what is called commando crawling, progress to getting up on their hands and knees and rocking back and forth, and finally take off like a bullet. The whole process could take a few days to several months. There are babies who develop a scooting process on their bottoms instead of crawling and some skip crawling completely and go to walking. We would only worry about a baby if they did not have enough strength to push up into a crawling position by the time they were about 9-12 months of age.

Walking: For most parents—and I was no exception—walking is the high mark in their baby's development. Those first steps are the stage most looked forward to and the one most cherished by parents. If everything is missed before and after, this is the "step" everyone wants to catch on film or tape and immortalize. It is also the one developmental step everyone turns into bragging rights and wants their child to do earlier than everyone else's child. Most babies will start off standing while holding on to their parent's hands as early as six months. Developmentally this skill just means their legs are strong enough to hold up their body weight since the parent is doing the balancing for them by holding their hands. Although this will help build up the strength in their legs needed for walking, this does not necessarily mean they soon will be walking. I commonly quote to parents that a baby will normally walk on their own somewhere between nine and 18 months. About half of the babies will walk by the time they are a year old. If they are 18 months and are not making any progress toward walking, pediatricians start to get worried about a developmental delay. The normal progression toward walking on their own will start with them pulling up against a couch or table. The next step is cruising, where they walk along a piece of furniture while holding on for dear life. They then will start letting go and standing on their own and will even stand up in the middle of the floor without holding on to anything. The next step is a few tottering steps which is then quickly followed by them running a hundred yard dash. I tell parents it is usually about one month from the time they start cruising until they are walking on their own. This is not a hard and fast rule, since some babies seem to be braver than others and some are more cautious and content to just hang on. If your baby is cruising well they probably have all the skills they need to walk on their own, they just lack the courage or desire. They will get there soon enough and then you will want to increase your anxiety medicine.

Going up and down stairs: It is hard to put a timeline on these skills, as they will vary considerably depending on the age your baby learns to crawl and walk. It also makes sense the baby will want to get flat surfaces figured out first. What will surprise you is how fast your baby will go from first learning to walk to climbing the stairs and trying to kill itself. Babies will first learn to crawl and walk up stairs well before they learn to go downstairs. (I have always thought this area is the one where the developmental order is backwards (for the well-being of the baby). This will of course lead to some dangers, since what goes up must come down. Gravity is sometimes a very hard and painful lesson for your little toddler. Given most babies will walk by themselves by 18 months, most babies are going to be going up stairs by this time as well. They will first need to hold a hand and then will progress to using the wall or handrail. It is not a concern if your baby cannot go upstairs by the age of two without holding on to something. To going downstairs they will start by scooting on their bottoms and then progress to dangerously tottering down by foot. Going downstairs will usually trail going upstairs by two or more months. It is completely fine, and probably a good idea, if your baby has never gone down a flight of stairs by themselves by the time they are two.

Talking: Parents are always in a hurry for their baby to talk, unless they have other children, and then they realize silence is golden and should last as long as possible. There is a huge range in the normal acquisition of language and I will try to touch on some of this. First, we will go through the normal development of language, then the normal ages each happens, what can cause variations in language development and when we get worried speech is not developing appropriately.

The first speech a baby makes is in the form of a cry and is going to happen soon after their first breath. You will soon become attuned to this form of speaking and realize all cries are not created equal. You will find your baby has a different cry for hunger, pain, sleepiness, fear, and to get your attention. I wish I could teach you this language, but it varies greatly from baby to baby. Thank goodness for the maternal or paternal instincts we were born with. The next stage of language will be gurgling noises the baby makes with its tongue, lips, and nose. Sounds then progress to oohs and goos that sound like they are practicing their vowel sounds. The next step is the addition of consonant sounds combined with the vowels, which is when you will start to hear things like words. These words will be the da-da, ma-ma, ba-ba variety and will be accompanied by some excited and competitive parents. The last stage will be where actual words with meaning start to appear. During this last stage babies will add words to their vocabulary and start to experiment with different sounds of the words to mean demands, statements or questions. As this stage progresses the baby starts to combine words to give them even more meaning and truly begins to speak.

The age ranges for the acquisition of language are only estimations. This estimation disclaimer is something commonly left out of parenting books. There are very few absolutes in childhood development and I will mention them as they pertain to language. Babies should start to cry after birth. This is an absolute and if they are not crying the pediatrician needs to find out why. The reasons could vary from not breathing to a condition affecting the vocal cords, and this is something the doctor will find out at a rapid rate of speed. The variations in the sound of crying are often heard soon after birth although you will find your instinctive interpretation may lag behind. Gurgling sounds start around the time a baby learns to smile and laugh, or around six to 12 weeks of age. The vowels follow with most babies cooing in the range of two to four months. The consonant sounds show up from five to nine months and so too are the claims the baby has spoken its first word. By the time a baby is one year of age they will usually have at least two to three words that are real words and have distinct meanings. The 15 month old toddler will usually have between five and 10 words. The 18-month child will have between 10 to 20 words. Most babies really take off between 18 and 24 months and will have up to several hundred words they will link together in two and three word sentences by their second birthday.

There are always variations to the norm and these variations can range from normal things that can be easily explained and addressed to problems needing to be pinpointed and taken care of by an appropriate means. There are some normal variations we see happen all the time. We find girls tend to talk earlier than boys. First-born children acquire words faster than subsequent children. Babies exposed to other babies and children tend to talk earlier than children who stay at home and are not around other children. Twins also tend to talk a little slower, at least in a language their parents can understand, but this is thought to be because they invent their own language to communicate between themselves. Some of the problems can cause delays in speech and include the following: problems in hearing, which could be caused by deafness or temporary problems like ear infections;

severe illnesses which lead to prolonged hospitalizations, such as premature babies or illnesses or injuries leading to prolonged intubation or sedation; and Pervasive Developmental Delay, commonly known as autism which can lead to other problems.

With all the above being said, when is your pediatrician going to get worried? We get worried if the baby does not cry after birth. This would not be normal and is something we would want to find a cause of. Some of the things we would check for if this happened would be to make sure the baby was breathing and not acutely ill. We would make sure the vocal cords were working properly; something we would suspect if the baby was acting like they were crying, but no sound was coming out. Finally we would worry something might not be right in the baby's brain so we would order some tests to look at the brain such as a CT. The next time your pediatrician would worry about speech development is around four to six months if a baby was not making vowel sounds or had stopped making vowel sounds. This could indicate your baby is not hearing well and would prompt them to do a hearing evaluation. The next stage that may cause your pediatrician to worry is when they are two years old and make no attempt to put words together or are not acquiring new words at a rapid rate. This is the time a speech evaluation would be ordered by a speech therapist. This is also one of the times more questions would be asked to evaluate for autism.

Your baby learning to talk is going to be an enjoyable time. It will also be a very short period of enjoyment. It will not take long before they are asking "why?" about everything, answering "no!" to all your questions, and claiming everything is "mine!" This is when you will believe the old adage, "silence is golden".

Know colors: There is a good chance your child will know at least one color by the time they are two years old. They will know more by the time they are three, however they may call every color the same thing. Every child has a different color, Dalton's was green. The funny thing is most of them when asked to go get a particular color will pick out the right one. This is one developmental milestone you can work on with your baby, but it means nothing if they do not know colors by the time they are two.

Know shapes: This is another one of the developmental milestones you want to start working on with your baby after they are one year old, but they are not necessarily expected to learn them by the time they are two. There will be babies who know shapes by the time they are two, but there are also babies reading by the age of two. Do not worry about them being delayed, just keep practicing by repetition.

Stack blocks: The question about block stacking is one that gets asked in office visits as a way to assess fine motor skills. The question itself will be, "How many blocks can your child stack on top of each other?" Your answer may depend on whether you have ever given your child blocks to play with. The age at which stacking blocks usually happens is as follows:

2 blocks by 15-21 months of age

4 blocks by 17-24 months of age

6 blocks by 18-36 months of age

8 blocks by 24-36 months of age

What happens if your child does not stack blocks? Then it is time to assess fine-motor skills other ways. Assessing how your child picks things up and if they can get objects out of a basket or put things in a box is a way of checking their fine-motor skills. If the baby is not developing fine-motor skills in an appropriate time then they may be referred to an occupational therapist. The therapist will then thoroughly evaluate your child to determine if a delay exists and then formulate a plan if needed to get your child's development up to age-specific levels.

Learn patty cake: I put this in here just to be obstinate. Your baby should not really know how to do the motions for the patty cake song in their first two years of life. The reason I have included this topic is so I can tell you a story. I have always thought the patty cake motions and song were silly, therefore I did not teach them to Dalton. One day at his daycare they were doing developmental assessments and we received a note saying he was delayed. I was surprised since I was a pediatrician and had not noticed any delays nor had his regular pediatrician. When we asked what area he was delayed in we learned it was his lack of ability to play patty cake. Sometimes children do not meet a certain milestone just because their parents have not taught them it.

Potty train: I know you wish this was a normal developmental milestone in the first two years, but it is not. Some of you will be lucky, thanks to the alignment of the planets that your child will be potty trained before they are two years of age. You could buy some help books, punish your child, practice elimination communication or any other of the numerous voodoo ideas out there but most of you will still be waiting until after they are two for your child to be potty trained. If your beloved child happens to be a girl, you will be more likely to be in the lucky group as girls having an average age of potty training around the age of two. If you have a boy who is an early potty trainer before two years old you have been very good. The average age for a little boy to potty train is three years old. Regardless of the age of your child's potty training the only thing it really means is you get to change more diapers and it's a good measure of how stubborn your child is.

It is time to start potty training when your child can start to control how often they are peeing and pooping and they show an interest in the toilet or at least a disinterest in their diaper being messy. Girls are easier to potty train because they do not like to be dirty and they love to please their parents. Boys are harder to potty train because they care less if they are dirty and they have better things to do than make their parents happy. I often tell parents never force a little girl to sit on the potty because they are little women and it is only a good idea if it is their idea. When they think it is a good idea, relegate yourself to a cheerleading position and make the potty available and heap on the praise, they will do the rest. If you have a little boy, you almost need to potty train them by gunpoint (dear American Academy of Pediatrics, I did not mean that literally). In the case of a little boy you are just going to have to start taking them to the bathroom and have them try. You may be doing this a couple of times an hour. You will eventually get them there when they have to go. Cheer when it happens and keep it up. They will eventually get the hang of going to the bathroom (getting them to get it in the toilet is a whole different story). For both girls and boys, peeing in the toilet is going to come before the pooping in the toilet (yes I know, it would be nice if it was the other way around).

CHAPTER 19

Diseases

"Doctor, she isn't so sick, but we need to get her better before she gives it to her dad because it's too much work to take care of him."

This chapter is by no means meant to be a medical text. It simply describe in terms most people can understand what some of the common diseases little ones will come in contact with during their first two years. There will be multiple times your friends are going to tell you they think your little baby may have this or that and this is a resource to look up the disease and see if it truly sounds like what your baby's symptoms are. You will also get little notes from daycare saying there is a certain disease in the classroom and using this chapter you will know what to look for as far as symptoms.

Chances are if you are referring to these chapters you are scared because your little one is sick. First, try to calm down; babies are going to get sick many times these first two years and they are tougher than we give them credit. Second, be glad we live in these modern times where most of these illnesses are treatable with modern medicine. Third, just remember as hard as it is to take care of your baby when they are sick, it is still easier than taking care of their daddy when he feels bad.

Chickenpox: Everybody knows about chickenpox right? Probably not so much anymore as most adults have not seen a case since they were a child and most of the daycare workers have not seen a real case. Because of this pediatricians see bunches of rashes people are worried might be chickenpox. Chickenpox is rarely seen in babies less than six months old because antibodies they get from their mother while she was pregnant protect them. Most cases of natural chickenpox seen these days are seen in babies between the ages of six months and one year. At one year, babies get a vaccine against chickenpox and we do not see many cases after the vaccine. The symptoms of chickenpox are fever and cold like symptoms for the first day followed by the rash. The chickenpox rash starts off as a red spot then a clear blister in the middle and finally over the next several hours the clear fluid in the blisters turns white. The spots become very itchy and you have a very miserable, itchy baby. Besides the miserably itchy rash the most common problem with chickenpox is the spot getting infected from all the scratching. Natural chickenpox can last 7-21 days during which time they are contagious the whole time. People wonder why we vaccinate against chickenpox since we all used to get it and we turned out fine. But they do not realize about 100 children die every year from complications of chickenpox. When I was in medical school I was against the chickenpox vaccine and even gave a little presentation about why I thought it should not be given. After I had a little six-year-old die from an overwhelming infection from chickenpox and I changed my mind. It only takes one child's death to make you realize how severe it can be.

Conjunctivitis: Conjunctivitis is the inflammation of the conjunctiva and is commonly known as pinkeye. The conjunctiva is the lining of the inside of the eyelid and the outer surface of the eyeball. It can become inflamed due to irritation from an object scratching against it, chemical or environmental irritants, allergies, viral infections or bacterial infections. Most of the time, you are going to need to talk to your doctor's office to figure out what the cause of your baby's red eye might be. Some infections of the eye can be serious and can threaten vision. Here are some of the most common offenders causing irritation to your little one's eyes:

Irritation by objects: By far the most common irritant is going to be their finger or their nail. This could range from just a minor little poke to the eye to a corneal abrasion where they scratch the cornea of their eye. A corneal abrasion is very painful and will cause a very teary eye and a crying baby. It needs to be followed by a visit to the doctor for pain control and to make sure it heals properly. Other common objects are going to be eyelashes, dust, or anything small that might be knocked into the eye while they happen to be looking up.

Chemical or environmental irritants: The first time you may encounter this type of irritation is in the hospital. The eye ointment place in baby's eyes to prevent gonorrhea can cause irritation and a red eye in the newborn. Other irritants would be household cleaning supplies the toddler happens to get a hold of and pour into their eye. **CALL POISON CONTROL ASAP FOR INSTRUCTIONS!** Cigarette smoke is another very common irritant leading to red eyes in babies.

Allergic conjunctivitis: Seasonal allergies can start in the first two years of life and can lead to red and puffy eyes. The red eyes will usually be accompanied by other allergy symptoms and will usually cause itchy eyes that tend to drain clear tears. If this becomes troublesome to your baby then give your doctor a call and ask what they recommend.

Viral conjunctivitis: Many different viruses such as influenza, Respiratory Syncytial Virus (RSV), and the viruses causing upper respiratory infections (URI) can cause conjunctivitis. The eyes can be red, scratchy and drain clear to thick discharge that looks like snot. It is sometimes hard even for your doctor to tell the difference between viral and bacterial conjunctivitis. If it persists for longer than a couple of days and is getting worse it is time to see your doctor. The most worrisome of the viruses causing conjunctivitis is herpes type I and II. These can lead to scarring of the cornea if not properly treated. If there are blisters around the eye or if the baby or toddler is crying in pain they need to be seen right away.

Bacterial conjunctivitis: In the newborn period the bacteria we worry the most about are gonorrhea and Chlamydia. These are two very common sexually transmitted diseases infected mothers can pass to their babies via the birth canal. These need to be treated immediately to prevent vision problems and even blindness. Other bacteria acquired from the birth canal can also lead to conjunctivitis, but are not as serious. Outside of the newborn period the usual culprits are the bacteria living in the nose and throat. These are the same bacteria causing ear infections and sinus infections.

Croup: Croup is a cold virus that is a little different from your average cold. It tends to be one of the first viruses of winter and is most commonly caused by a virus called *parainfluenza*. It has a very characteristic cough that sounds very hoarse and like a barking seal. It is usually worse at night between the hours of 9 p.m. and 5-6 a.m. This is when your body's natural steroid is at its lowest point and swelling is at its highest point. The medical term for croup is laryngotracheobronchitis and the most important part of the name is the "laryngo" part. This is where the vocal cords are and the narrowest part of the airway. Swelling occurring at this level causes the hoarse "barky" cough and if the swelling gets severe enough it can lead to stridor. Stridor is a wheezing sound that happens when the baby breathes in. This means the baby is having a hard time getting the air in and as the air goes through the narrowing it makes a wheezing sound. If your baby has the barky cough or stridor the first thing you want to do is put a humidifier or vaporizer by their bed or you may want to steam up the bathroom with a hot shower and let them breathe the steam. This will often help but if it does not and they continue to have stridor or problems breathing you need to get to your doctor or the emergency room right away. The doctors can administer a special breathing treatment with a medicine known as racemic epinephrine and possibly give an oral or injectable steroid. Every once in a while, a baby will be bad enough they will need to be admitted to the hospital for more frequent steroids, breathing treatments or oxygen.

Ear Infection: Ear infections are a common bacterial infection affecting little ones. Ear infections are usually secondary infections. This means they usually happen in the middle or end of another illness or condition like colds or allergies. Colds or allergies cause swelling of the lining of the nose and throat and can swell the tissues lining the tube connecting the middle ear to the throat closed and allow fluid to accumulate in the middle ear and get infected. The bacteria causing ear infections are commonly the infant's own bacteria and normally found in their nose and throat. Ear infections will present with a baby who is fussy, has fever, a decreased appetite and pulling at their ear. Ear infections can be either viral or bacterial. When you suspect ear infections you should see your pediatrician. Your baby's doctor will determine what the likelihood of the infection being bacterial is and treat with either an antibiotic or pain medication.

Fifth's Disease: Another one of those pesky little rash-causing baby viruses. It received its name because it was the fifth infectious rash causing viruses (funnily enough the others are not known by their number). It is caused by the human parvovirus B19. This little virus usually is mild and known mostly for its rash. It causes a bright red rash on the cheeks that looks like the little one has been slapped across the face (which is why it is known commonly as "Slapped Cheek Syndrome"). After the rash shows up on the cheeks they may get a little lace-like rash on their arms and legs. If the little person has a fever at all it will be very low and usually less than 101 degrees. They might have a slight runny nose and maybe a slightly sore throat but nothing else. By the time you see the bright red cheeks they are no longer contagious so there is no use keeping them out of daycare or school. There is no treatment to give or do at home. Pregnant women exposed to fifth's disease need to notify their obstetrician immediately because of the risk of pregnancy complications.

Hand-Foot-Mouth Disease: This name was originally called Hand-Hoof-and Mouth Disease until the doctors agreed babies do not really have hooves and it might be better to refer to them as feet. This is a viral infection commonly caused by *coxsackievirus*, and is most common in the warmer months of the year. It is characterized by fever, blisters in the mouth that can be on the gums, tongue and roof of mouth, and a rash appearing as little red bumps or small blisters found anywhere on the body, but is different than most by being found on the palms of the hands and the soles of the feet. We try to encourage pushing fluids to prevent dehydration, giving meds like acetaminophen or ibuprofen for pain or fever. Check with your personal pediatrician to see if there are any other pain remedies they recommend.

Herpes Simplex: Herpes simplex comes as type I and type II. Herpes simplex type II is commonly called genital herpes and type I is what is commonly referred to as a cold sore. Herpes simplex II can be transmitted to babies by an infected mother and can cause some very serious conditions for a newborn, but for this book we are going to discuss type I. First of all let me give you this warning: **NEVER LET ANYONE KISS YOUR NEWBORN WHO HAS A COLD SORE!** People don't realize the virus in a cold sore can cause a life threatening illness in a baby that can affect their eyes, skin, and brain. Most people who are exposed to herpes simplex I will never know it and never break out in a cold sore. Some of the unfortunate little ones who are exposed to a cold sore will develop a condition known as herpetic gingivostomatitis (medical code for miserable little baby). This will cause symptoms such as a fever, a fussy baby who refuses to eat or drink, and probably drooling. When you look inside their mouth you see blisters on their tongue, lips, gums, or the back of their throat. I have seen babies with literally hundreds of blisters in their mouth. The main thing we worry about is a baby getting dehydrated from not drinking enough. Some babies will need I.V. fluids and if they are old enough your pediatrician may prescribe antiviral medicines, medicines to coat or soothe the sores and sometime even prescription pain medications. While they have the blisters, they are very contagious and should not be around other children, especially newborns.

Influenza: This is what you hear called the flu. We need to start off clearing up a common misconception we all hear frequently. The flu has nothing to do with vomiting and diarrhea. The flu is a severe cold with coughing, fever, runny nose, sneezing, watery eyes, aching, and fatigue. The thing that makes the flu stand out from other cold viruses is the severity of all the symptoms. The fever is usually very high between 101-104 degrees Fahrenheit. The cough is very deep and productive and is usually worse on days 3-6. The congestion and runny nose make it hard to breathe. The flu causes intense myalgias which means your muscles hurt all over. It is not uncommon for little ones to feel so bad they moan in their sleep. They tend to look like you sucked half the life out of them and their little eyes are so watery it looks like they are crying even when they are not. The flu is notorious for leading to secondary infections like ear infections, sinus infections and pneumonia. There are medications to treat the flu and alter its normal course if caught early, so early diagnosis is a helpful thing. If you feel your little one has the flu watch closely for signs of worsening and secondary infections. If your baby is older than six months old we recommend yearly flu vaccines.

Meningitis: Meningitis is an inflammation of the meninges. This is the most feared condition by your pediatrician and the one we dread hearing about and finding. Let's start by describing what it is, what causes it, what meningitis does, and what can be done. The meninges are the lining of the brain and spinal cord. Meningitis just means this lining is upset and inflamed. This inflammation will cause symptoms such as fever, headache, neck stiffness, vomiting and make you feel like you are going to die. The problem with meningitis in a little baby is they will not always show the typical symptoms of meningitis until they are 18 months old. That is why your pediatrician is always thinking about and trying to rule out meningitis in their head when your baby comes into the office sick.

Meningitis can be caused by bacteria and viruses most commonly, but is also occasionally caused by tuberculosis and yeast in severely immuno-compromised people. The symptoms will be the same regardless of the cause, but of course the treatments are going to be very different. The test for meningitis is one of the most feared and dreaded by parents and is called a spinal tap or lumbar puncture. Now many moms will have had an experience with a similar procedure because most of them will have had a spinal or epidural for pain during delivery. A lumbar puncture is technically much easier on a baby, but no easier on the parent of the baby. The spinal fluid is sent for some tests and cultures and from those it is determined what type of meningitis the baby has. All babies less than two months old with a fever are just assumed to have meningitis until the culture is negative and are put in the hospital for at least two days. All children less than two months with tests indicating the baby has a type of meningitis are going to be put in the hospital on antibiotics until the doctors make sure the infection is not caused by a bacteria. There are different bacteria and viruses that can cause meningitis, but this is really for the medical people to deal with. The bottom line for you as the parent is meningitis is bad and you do not want your baby to have it.

Pneumonia: Pneumonia is an infection of the lungs and can be caused by bacteria, viruses, and fungi. Usually when people discuss pneumonia they are talking about bacterial pneumonia. Most pneumonia is a secondary infection, just like ear infections and sinus infections, and is largely caused by the same kinds of bacteria. Because the same kinds of bacteria are the cause, the types of antibiotics are similar as well. The symptoms of pneumonia usually occur in the middle or end of a cold when all of a sudden the little one gets a high fever usually over 101 degrees, their cough may or may not get worse, they may have decreased appetite, vomiting and look very sick. If you suspect pneumonia, you should always see your pediatrician as soon as possible. Your doctor may be able to hear the pneumonia with their stethoscope, but often the baby is screaming, crying and thrashing around so much they may just suspect pneumonia and order a chest x-ray. Your baby's age, whether they are vomiting, how severe the pneumonia is, and how your baby looks will determine whether they treat them with antibiotics at home or put them in the hospital for a few days. Babies who get pneumonia over and over will need a work-up to find out why it is happening. Things the doctor will consider are immune problems, asthma, cystic fibrosis and aspirations (choking on food or milk and sucking it into the lungs).

Roseola: You got to love roseola because once you know the diagnosis the illness is done. This is a viral infection most babies will have had by the time they are three years of age. Its only symptom in the beginning is fever and fussiness. The fever can be fairly high and with no other symptoms. Many babies will end up having a lot of lab work done to make sure they do not have any serious illness. After about the third day of illness the fever goes away and the baby breaks out in a red poke-a-dot rash all over their body and the disease is done. The baby is contagious while they have the fever, but not after they break out in the rash. The rash can last 2-5 days and then goes away. The rash tends to get brighter when the baby gets warm like after baths or playing.

Rotavirus: Rotavirus is a virus that typically happens in late winter or early spring. This virus causes severe vomiting and diarrhea. I like to call it rota-rooter virus because it cleans everything out of the plumbing. It causes very watery, foul smelling, green diarrhea that shoots out of their little bottom like a fountain. By definition, diarrhea is more than six stools per day and it is not uncommon for little babies to have as many as 20 dirty diapers per day. The danger of rotavirus is severe dehydration. The good news is we now have vaccines for rotavirus, which are making a huge impact on how severe this illness is. See Chapter 20 for the signs of dehydration and if you suspect dehydration see your doctor or the emergency room immediately. To treat rotavirus we routinely get you to stop all dairy in the baby's diet for a few days and go to a lacto-free formula. If eating solid foods, things like toast, cereal, applesauce, and potatoes will help slow stools down. If you are worried always give your pediatrician a call for more advice.

Respiratory Syncytial Virus (RSV): RSV in pediatrics is three letters causing about as much fear as the letters IRS does to accountants. RSV is a cold virus, which likes to attack the smallest airways of the lungs. Think of a tree and its system of branches and consider that if it were hollow the bronchioles would be the branch holding the leaves on the tree. RSV attacks the lining of the bronchioles. I like to describe it as like peeling sunburn and the dead skin then gets in and blocks the airway (it's a little more complicated than that, but it makes for a good visual). With all that stuff in the way you can imagine how it would be hard to breathe and if you were trying to cough it up you may get an idea of how terrible the cough would sound. I like to describe their breathing as sounding like a broken washing machine. This disease tends to show up in the winter months with a peak from November to February. It is much worse the smaller the baby, with the premature babies being the hardest hit. Many babies are admitted to hospitals every year because of respiratory distress secondary to RSV. Most pediatric offices will be able to test for this virus in their office by doing a simple nasal swab. They will get the answer from the swab in about 10 minutes. Treatments at home mostly consist of sucking out the baby's nose, running a vaporizer or humidifier in their room, pushing fluids, and lots of love. When babies start to work very hard to breathe by having retractions (pulling dents in their skin between the ribs, or under the ribcage), or breathing very fast, it is time to go to your doctor's office or an emergency room. The doctor may give your baby different types of breathing treatments, some better nasal suction, or give your baby oxygen if needed.

All children will get RSV eventually with about 80 percent getting an infection by the time they are three years old. You will hear people say RSV causes asthma, which is not true. It is true that if you were meant to develop asthma you may start to have problems while infected with RSV. This virus is most scary for babies less than six months old, but is not fun for any babies less than two years old.

Sepsis: Sepsis is a medical term that means an overwhelming bacterial infection of the body, which leads to important body functions to shut down. As a parent you are going to hear this term most frequently when your doctor uses the term "rule out sepsis work-up". This usually means your baby has a fever and looks sick, but no reason for this has been found in their examination. This makes your doctor worry there is a bacteria infecting an area that is not as easy to look at such as a urinary tract infection, bacteria in the blood (called bacteremia), or bacteria in the fluid around the brain and spinal cord (called meningitis). A "rule-out-sepsis" work-up includes blood work, urinalysis and often a spinal tap. Most of these babies will be started on antibiotics either by a shot or by an I.V. and put in the hospital until they know what is going on.

Sinusitis: Sinusitis is something parents think their baby has every time they have a cold and their snot turns yellow or green. Yellow or green snot does not mean anything except their snot has some color to it. The signs of a sinus infection in a baby are a cough that lasts longer than 10 days that happens only when they lie down or first get up. They usually have little to no fever. Every time your baby has a cough lasting longer than 10 days it is a good idea to have them looked at by your doctor. Sinus infections will be treated with antibiotics if your doctor feels the cause is bacterial.

Strep Throat: Strep throat is one of the most common bacterial infections you will see in children because it is contagious. Strep throat is spread by contact with the bacteria found in infected people's spit. Therefore it is most commonly spread by drinking after infected people, eating after infected people, kissing infected people or putting things in your mouth which have been in someone else's mouth who was infected (all things that little kiddos like to do all the time). It is uncommon to see strep throat in babies less than nine months old just because of the method of transfer, but I have seen them get it from older siblings who sometimes steal their pacifier, bottle or sippy cup.

The biggest symptoms of strep throat are going to be fever, sore throat, headache, and abdominal pain. In the little ones who still cannot tell you what is bothering them you will usually see fever, decreased appetite, drooling, fussiness and sometime vomiting. You may notice your baby's throat looks red if you can get them to open their mouth wide enough to get a look inside (try it sometime and you will have a new appreciation for my job). Sometimes you can see a red, bumpy rash on their body too. Your doctor is usually going to make the diagnosis by a throat swab in the office where they may do a rapid test or send the swab for culture. Strep throat is usually treated with antibiotics in the penicillin family unless your child is allergic to penicillin and it can be given by mouth or by a shot. The way it is treated is going to depend a lot on how your child is doing. If they are vomiting prepare yourself for a shot. The real reason we treat strep throat is to decrease the spread of the disease and to prevent rheumatic fever. Rheumatic fever is what happens when your body fights off strep with antibodies it makes itself, but the antibodies start to attack parts of your body, of which the most serious is the valves of your heart (not a good thing to happen). Children with strep throat are usually considered contagious until they have been on antibiotics for 24 hours.

Thrush: This is a very common yeast infection little babies commonly acquire. In all honestly it is not really an infection it is more a yeast overgrowth. Everyone has yeast, but there are certain conditions allowing it to overgrow. The major cause is just being a baby and having an immature immune system. Another common cause is being on antibiotics as the antibiotics do away with the bacteria and the yeast has no competition and it overgrows. The thrush will look bright white and will typically be stuck to the roof of the mouth, side of the mouth and on the tongue. The baby may be fussy because the yeast does cause some pain. Thrush is usually treated with an antifungal medication like nystatin. Pediatricians recommend boiling pacifiers and nipples until the mouth is clear. It the baby is breastfed; mom's nipples will also need to be treated.

Upper Respiratory Infection (URI): This sounds like something very serious and very medical does it not? URI is medical lingo for a cold; yep the common head cold you have been getting every winter since you were a little kid. Colds are caused by a collection of viruses called the rhinoviruses and coronoviruses (like you would ever care what they were called). There are over 200 of these little monsters and they like to change over time insuring you will never stop getting colds your entire life. These are the most common infectious diseases in humans with the average child getting 6-12 per year and adults getting 2-4 per year (which seems to go up quite a bit when you have sick kids in your house).

The most common symptoms with the common cold are cough, sore throat, runny nose, congestion and fever. Some of the highest fevers we see in pediatrics can happen with the common cold. The most effective treatments for the common cold are getting plenty of fluids, resting, and acetaminophen or ibuprofen for the fever and aches and pains (chicken noodle soup doesn't hurt). Colds are spread by respiratory droplets being shot out of the infected person's nose and mouth and ending up in your nose, mouth or eyes (nice huh?). The only proven way to cut down on colds is frequent hand washing, keeping your hands away from your eyes or mouth, and of course staying away from virus spewing sick people.

The normal progression of a cold is to feel a little achy or tired, start running a fever if you are going to get one, congestion and sore throat and then finally to start coughing your bloody head off. You need to bring your little one to the doctor if the fever lasts longer than three days, if the fever goes away for more than 24 hours and then comes back in the middle or end of the cold, if your little one has a hard time breathing, or if they start acting like they are in any pain.

Urinary Tract Infection (UTI): UTI comes in two different varieties. The more common and less severe is the bladder infection (which we in the snotty medical community would call cystitis) and the less common, but much more severe kidney infection (which the snobs would call pyelonephritis). Neither of the two is very nice to have but let's talk about the different presentations and causes of both of them.

Cystitis: (does that make me a snob?) Cystitis is an irritation of the bladder. It can be due to an infection by bacteria or virus, but most commonly bacteria. The most common bacteria causing cystitis is E. coli (it is called *Escherichia coli*, but let's be honest that just doesn't roll off the tongue). E. coli usually comes from the baby's poop and just ends up in the wrong spot. This happens more commonly in little girls just because of the difference in plumbing (with the little girls the bacteria just has a shorter distance to travel to cause problems). This is going to cause your baby to hurt when they pee. The problem for you is knowing it hurts when they pee. It is more likely your pediatrician will notice when you bring your baby in because they are fussy and crying intermittently. Sometimes parents will notice a foul smell to the urine, a different color or blood in the front part of the diaper. Just to warn you, until a baby is potty trained most urine is going to be obtained by a urinary catheterization. This sounds like a terrible thing, but it is done under sterile conditions by people who do it everyday and is done with baby-sized catheters. You will sometimes hear of urine being caught by a "bag". I was always taught "bags are for garbage" and I never use them because you always end up with bacteria from their bottom and you might be treating a urinary tract infection that is not really there. Once a urinary tract infection is diagnosed and the doctor is sure it is cystitis the baby is put on antibiotics and typically gets better in a few days. Most doctors will send the urine for a culture to make sure the antibiotic they are using will work and to make sure what bacteria it is they are treating.

Pyelonephritis: Pyelonephritis is an infection of the kidney. This type of urinary tract infection is very serious and if untreated could lead to severe damage to the kidney and even death. It is usually caused by the same type of bacteria as the less severe cystitis but causes much worse illness. With pyelonephritis you see symptoms of high fever, chills, vomiting, back pain, painful urination, and they also look and feel really sick. Again most of the little ones we are talking about in this book cannot talk so we are looking for this in babies with fever, fussiness and vomiting. Again the diagnosis is usually made by performing a urinary catheterization in babies who are not potty trained. A diagnosis of pyelonephritis is usually going to get you some additional blood tests and most likely a little stay in the hospital for some I.V. antibiotics until your little one's fever is gone. Your doctor should also order a couple of tests once your baby is feeling better to determine why the bacteria was able to get up to the kidney. The two tests they should order are an ultrasound of the kidney to make sure it looks good, is the right size and is where it is supposed to be; and a voiding cystourethrogram (or a VCUG — thank goodness for abbreviations) which is where the baby has a urinary catheterization done and dye is injected into the bladder to make sure nothing is wrong with the plumbing and urine is not going a direction it's not supposed to go. The dye is used to look for malformations that could require surgery to fix. The most common abnormality found is urinary reflux, which is discussed, in the next chapter.

CHAPTER 20

Medical conditions

"Yes, Mrs. Charles, I'm sure there isn't a disease
called 'Nincumpoop Syndrome'."

I n the last chapter we talked about diseases and now we are talking about conditions, so what is the difference? Diseases are things caused by something infectious. The medical conditions are things that happen that are not necessarily infectious, but are still not right and in many cases suck more and for a longer time. Just like in the last chapter this is not going to give you enough information to go out and start a pediatric office. It hopefully will be a reference you can look at to put these conditions in terms you can understand so you can ask your doctor better questions and know why certain things are being done. Sometimes it is just nice to know your doctor does know what they are talking about and somebody out there writing a book would have done the same thing. Just know your baby is not the only one these things are going to happen to. These are discussions you will need to have with your baby's doctor. There are never simple answers why these conditions occur or how they are treated.

Allergies: In this category we are talking about seasonal and environmental allergies. At around the age of six months babies can start to develop allergies to the things around them all the time, these things commonly include allergies to pets, dust mites, molds and things found around the house. After the first year they can start to have allergies to seasonal things like pollen, grass, molds and ragweed. I like to describe allergies as being a tree with two big branches. On one branch we have the histamine side that causes the symptoms of watery eyes, runny nose, sneezing, coughing and itching. On the other branch we have the inflammatory symptoms which cause swelling and leads to the nasal congestion, sinus pressure, headaches, and secondary infections like ear and sinus infections. Babies and big people can have symptoms on one branch or the other or both at the same time. The histamine side of the tree is usually treated with antihistamines, and the inflammatory side is treated with nasal steroids and medications called leukotriene modifiers (such fancy words). If allergy symptoms become troublesome it is time to bother that pediatrician of yours and find out what they recommend using and the dose for your child. Allergy testing for babies less than two years old is not very useful except in cases where you suspect a specific allergen like dog or cat dander or a specific food such as shrimp. There are some allergies, which can be life threatening. Allergies to stings, medicines and food can lead to anaphylaxis.

Food Allergies: Food allergies can happen with all types of foods and the symptoms and cause can be hard to detect. One thing to remember is the sooner solid foods are introduced the more likely the baby is to develop food allergies. Babies born into families with a strong history of food allergies are recommended to hold off on solid foods until six months of age. The first food a baby could develop an allergy to is milk. Symptoms of milk protein allergies range from eczema, diarrhea, bloody stools, fussiness, vomiting and hives. The doctors often test stools for blood and depending on the severity and the symptoms your pediatrician may consult a pediatric specialist called a gastroenterologist (try saying that 10 times fast). Babies are often tried on specialty formulas made for babies with allergies to milk. These formulas are very expensive and should only be recommended and changed by your doctor. It often takes days to weeks to see the results of the change and if you are changing too fast it makes it hard for your doctor to figure out what is going on. Some of these babies could even end up getting a procedure to look into their intestine to see what is going on.

The next types of food allergies we start having pop up happen when we start introducing solid foods. Some of the most common foods to develop an allergy to are tree nuts, peanuts (bet you thought they were the same, but a peanut is not really a nut), shellfish, eggs, soybeans, wheat and fish. The symptoms of food allergies are itchy rashes like hives that are described later, eczema, abdominal pain, vomiting, diarrhea, shortness of breath and wheezing. If your child has sudden abdominal pain, wheezing and shortness of breath, they may have a special condition called anaphylaxis, which is life threatening and needs immediate emergency assistance (**CALL 911**). Any suspicion of allergy you should contact your pediatrician and get advice what to do and ways to prevent and treat in the future. The nice thing is most food allergies are outgrown by children except for nuts and shellfish that are not outgrown as often.

Eczema: Eczema is a very common skin rash little ones can have on their body. It tends to run in families with allergies and asthma. Eczema can sometimes be a sign of a food allergy and should be suspected if you have just added a new food. Eczema tends to be worse on the face and trunk during the first year of life and on the arms, legs and around joints after the first year. For most children eczema is worse during the winter months. Eczema tends to have flares that come and go and can be triggered by allergies, illnesses or staying wet. Most doctors recommend infrequent bathing in babies with eczema, using good lotions twice a day (by good we mean lotions commonly used by adults as baby lotion is mostly so babies don't smell like poop), and trying to keep them from scratching at the rash since digging makes it worse. Eczema comes in mild, moderate and severe forms, which range from a mild dry rash to a baby who looks like they are a burn victim. We often call eczema "the itch that rashes" because the more they scratch at it the worse it gets. Many of the modalities of controlling eczema involve trying to keep the baby from scratching their skin. If you baby is falling in the moderate to severe category its time to see the pediatrician and they may prescribe antihistamines for itching and prescription strength steroid creams.

Asthma: Asthma is a narrowing of the airways in your lungs causing you to have problems breathing. The narrowing of the airways is caused by a spasm or swelling, with swelling being the most common. Triggers for an asthma attack include viruses, allergies or irritants. The viruses are typical cold viruses. Allergies can be of the seasonal variety or an allergic reaction to medicines or foods. Irritants can include dust, smoke, perfumes, or pretty much anything that annoys your airways. The stages of an asthma attack are as follows: first it takes longer to get air out, second a wheeze develops as you breathe out, third wheezing occurs when breathing in and out as it worsens, fourth there is only wheezing when breathing in, and fifth and finally no wheeze because not enough air is moving back and forth to make any noise. What does all this mean to you as a parent? Probably not very much, but it is nice to know what the doctor is talking about when they are talking about the severity of an asthma attack. What you need to know about a baby who is less than two years old is they are going to be breathing fast, working hard to breathe, and you may hear them making a whistling sound when they are breathing. You may also see what are called retractions, which is where they are pulling in between their ribs, under their ribcage and above their clavicle. If your baby is wheezing you need to see a doctor as soon as possible, this is not something you want to wait several hours before being seen. This is one condition where it is always a good idea to go to the emergency room if it is happening at night.

Asthma often runs in families who have asthma, allergies and eczema. Your doctor is usually going to ask about a family history of asthma. For most babies they will eventually outgrow asthma, but this is one condition you want to take very serious because it can be life threatening. If your doctor recommends medicines be taken daily be sure and take them, if they recommend staying away from certain things, then it is a good idea to stay away from them. Sometimes you have to ask yourself who do I love more, my cigarettes (or whatever it is they are sensitive to), or my baby? (If your answer is not your baby you should stop reading this book and start reading one on how to set up an adoption). If you want to change your medicine it is time to go see your pediatrician and see what different medicines are available and get a plan of action.

Gastroesophageal Reflux Disease (GERD/ Reflux): Commonly known as reflux, this is where the contents of the stomach come up into the esophagus. The esophagus is the tube connecting your mouth to your stomach. By definition it is any substance (fluid or solid) going from the stomach into the esophagus. It can go a short distance or can go all the way to the mouth and induce vomiting. All babies have reflux. Every baby spitting up has just had an episode of reflux. For the most part, reflux in babies is normal and does not cause any problems. Doctors are going to be concerned if the common reflux starts to cause uncommon problems. The problem begins if the baby starts to spit up so much they are not growing, starts to have pain from the burning of their esophagus from the stomach acid going up where it is not supposed to go, or stops breathing and turning blue from not being able to breath around the obstruction of the substance being spit up. Babies will be weighed and measured at all their checkups and plotted on a growth curve. Those curves are something to help the pediatrician decide if the reflux is affecting the baby's growth. This is just one of the reasons it is important to keep all your well-baby appointments. A baby having pain from reflux will cry when eating, cry when spitting up, tend to be fussier generally and may arch their back while being unhappy. Of course if a baby is stopping breathing and turning blue you are going to notice it happening. If your baby is stopping breathing or turning blue, do not assume they are just having reflux, **CALL 911 NOW!** Do not think about anything else; do not call your mother, brother, sister or even your doctor for advice…**CALL 911!** Depending on the symptoms your baby is having your doctor may order some tests, may try some changes in feeding or positioning of your baby, may try some medications or even refer your baby to see a specialist.

Hives: Hives in medical lingo is known as urticaria (which is hard to say and even harder to spell, but I guess it sounds smart). These are reddish-colored blotches that can appear anywhere on the body. They are usually slightly elevated and the edges are usually a little darker than the center. It is hard to comprehend, but one hive or a hundred hives mean the same thing to a doctor. They are usually moving around and can't really stay in the same spot, if they do stay in the same spot for more than about a day it is not a hive. Hives can be caused by an allergy to something coming in contact with the skin or an allergy to something the baby ate such as food or medicines. Babies can break out in hives secondary to illnesses or stressors, from being in cold water, being out in the sunlight too long or for any number of reasons even your pediatrician cannot figure out (these reasons are called idiopathic which in my lingo means we are too big of an idiot to figure them out). You should always call your pediatrician to figure out what the cause was and what you need to do to help your little one. If your child has any wheezing, problems breathing, vomiting, or uncontrollable crying you need them to be seen as soon as possible...**CALL 911!** Some causes of hives may require a referral to a specialist for additional testing.

Apnea: Apnea is a pause in breathing lasting greater than 20 seconds. Try to hold your breath and count 1 Mississippi...2 Mississippi...3 Mississippi... etc. and you will get the idea it feels like forever. The other problem is they hardly ever say, "Hey Mom and Dad! Watch me I'm about to stop breathing so start doing the Mississippi counting thing." So just try to count when you notice them stopping breathing as they are usually going to do it more than once if it is truly apnea. This is another one of those emergency times for which you must **CALL 911! GO TO THE HOSPITAL!**

So what could be causing the apnea? It could be caused by a severe infection that could range from a blood infection, urinary tract infection, or meningitis. It could be caused by reflux. A baby can stop breathing if they are having a seizure, have had some kind of brain trauma or a brain malformation. They can also have what is called obstructive apnea from something getting in the way of their breathing like really big tonsils or adenoids. Because of this a baby having apnea is going to have tests to rule out infections, reflux and brain problems while they are in the emergency room or hospital.

Sudden Infant Death Syndrome (SIDS): SIDS, or Crib Death as it used to be called, is when a baby is found dead while it has been asleep. It is what we are worried about may happen when a child is having apnea. It was once recommended babies sleep on their bellies that was found to contribute to SIDS. Since the recommendations for babies to sleep on their backs started, the numbers of babies dying from SIDS has greatly reduced. We do know there are certain risk factors for SIDS, which can be identified, and babies can be watched closer and the risk factors removed. Babies at highest risk are male; aged one to six months (it being the highest between the second and third month); premature; low birth weight babies; of Black, American Indian, or Native Alaskan ethnicity; born to a mom using tobacco or drugs during pregnancy; exposed to second hand smoke; in a house that is too warm; born in the winter; and finally who've had a sibling who died of SIDS. The take home message would be put your baby to sleep on its back, do not use drugs, do not smoke, do not keep the house too hot and if you have had a baby who died of SIDS before, let your pediatrician know.

Colic: I would like to change the name colic to Crazy Parent Syndrome. The reason for my suggested change in name is colic falls into two categories: parents who are just crazy and think a baby is never supposed to cry or parents who will soon be crazy because a truly colicky baby will drive someone stark-raving mad. The definition of colic is a baby who cries non-stop for at least two hours for five out of seven days for at least two weeks. The best way I can personally describe a colic baby is one that screams like you were cutting off their finger. A colicky cry truly gets on your nerves. We do not really know what causes colic, but we think it has something to do with the intestinal tract since some of the interventions we have found that work have to do with manipulation of formulas or medicines affecting the gastrointestinal tract.

Babies with colic like to be moving constantly. I tell my parents you can diagnose colic by driving in the car; a baby with colic will be calm while driving and will start crying every time the car comes to a stop. I have had parents calm them down in swings, bouncy seats, and going for car rides. They also like what is called white noise which is static. I have had parents calm their little one down with static from radios or televisions, the sound of fans, vacuum cleaners (parents have burnt out the motor in their vacuum cleaner), and buying little machines to make white noise. You will need to talk to your pediatrician before you go crazy to see what he suggests trying to do to help your family. He may recommend a change in formula, have some other tricks up his sleeve and sometimes even medicine may be recommended.

Gas: Gas is simply air coming out of one end or the other. Most of the air going out is air they have previously swallowed. Babies swallow air while they are drinking their milk either by breastfeeding or bottle-feeding or while they are crying. Once air has been swallowed and gets into the stomach it will have to come back up the esophagus and exit as a burp or travel through the entire intestinal tract and exit as flatulence (fart, toot, poot, cut-the-cheese, pixie, let one loose, or whatever your parents called it). Just for the record I had never heard the whole pixie thing until my wife told me that is what she called them when she was a little girl. The average baby is going to pass gas 10-20 times per day. Gas can also be formed in the intestinal tract from the breakdown of food products.

Not all gas is normal and there can be things causing babies to have excessive gas. Excessive burping can be caused by swallowing too much air while eating because of a nipple not flowing right, or crying and swallowing air secondary to pain or colic. Flatulence can be abnormal because of problems with digestion such as lactose intolerance or an allergy to foods. Gas should not be painful since it is something normal that happens without them even noticing it. If your baby is crying do not just blame the gas as the gas may be happening because of what is causing the pain. Babies having excessive gas and pain should warrant a call to your pediatrician.

Failure to Thrive: Failure to thrive is the term you will hear pediatricians use if your baby is not growing the way they would predict. A baby's growth is plotted on curves to follow the baby's length, weight, and head circumference. If a baby's growth is not what the curves would predict then we need to figure out why. If the baby was large and the parents are pigmies then should not be a surprise when their growth starts to fall down the curve. If the baby's head starts to look small it would be nice to know everyone in the family has really small heads. There are many reasons why a baby might not grow the way we would predict but it should stimulate some questions by your pediatrician and maybe even some tests.

Urinary Reflux: Urinary reflux is where urine goes the wrong direction and flows from the bladder back up to the kidney. Urinary reflux can lead to urinary tract infections and long-term kidney damage. Urinary reflux is diagnosed using a test called a voiding cystourethrogram or VCUG. This test is done by injecting dye into the bladder and watching via x-ray to see where the dye goes. Urinary reflux is graded from I to V. Grade I reflux goes up into the tube connecting the kidney to the bladder which is known as the ureter. Grade II is where urine goes backwards all the way up the ureter to the kidney. Grade III is when the urine goes all the way up the ureter into the kidney and causes mild dilation of the kidney, which is called hydronephrosis. Grade IV is when the urine goes all the way up the ureter to the kidney and causes moderate dilation of the kidney. Grade V is when the dilation of the kidney is severe and the ureter is very swollen and kinked. Grade I and II are often watched over time and usually if urinary tract infections are prevented they will go away on their own. Grade III will go away on its own about half the time. Grade IV and V usually need surgery to fix. Most of the time if your baby is diagnosed with Grade III, IV or V reflux you will be referred to a pediatric urologist, which is a surgeon specializing in children's urinary tract surgeries.

Teething: All babies will get teeth. The symptoms that come along with getting them are called teething. How many symptoms they have will vary with every baby as does how long they will last and how severe they will be. First off know that extreme symptoms should not be blamed on teething. For example if your baby looks very sick then think about everything else before you blame their teeth. Symptoms attributed to teething include low grade fevers (never above 101), runny nose, drooling, chewing on things, not wanting to eat, sporadic choking sounding coughs, pulling on ears, and loose stools. Most commonly these symptoms are annoying at the most. If the baby is having a hard time with their teeth pediatricians will recommend acetaminophen, something cold or hard to chew on and lots of love. There are several homeopathic treatments available that are not routinely recommended by pediatricians for teething because of safety concerns. If you have lots of coughing, fevers higher than 101, and more than six stools per day you have an illness, not teething.

A baby's first tooth can come in any time between two months and 18 months old. About a half of the babies will have a tooth by the time they are six months old. About 80 percent of the time their first teeth will be the two bottom front teeth, followed by the four top front teeth, then the other two bottom front teeth, then the molars and the canine teeth coming in last. Top teeth seem to have more symptoms than the bottom teeth. We recommend just brushing teeth with a brush and water until they are one year of age and then using flavored fluorinated toothpaste after their first birthday. The pediatric dentists recommend their first dental visit one year after their first tooth, but I routinely recommend their first visit after they are two years of age.

Vomiting: Vomiting is different from spitting up. Think about spitting up being the amount to fill up maybe two or three teaspoons. When you can fill up small bowls then we are talking about vomiting. If you have vomiting and diarrhea then you most likely have a virus. If you have only vomiting then there are many things that could be the cause. If you have more than two episodes of vomiting and no diarrhea then it is probably time to call the doctor. Things important to think about are: does your baby have fever, are they urinating normally, are they awake and acting normal, and do they have any other symptoms like cough or crying? So what kinds of things is your doctor going to be thinking about? Terrible things like strep throat, pneumonia, meningitis, urinary tract infections, blood infections, intestinal obstructions, and probably at least a hundred other reasons causing vomiting. Now you understand why it is time to call a doctor; make them sweat and work out why your baby is vomiting as opposed to taking on that responsibility yourself.

So your doctor tells you your baby has a virus, now what do you do? Your doctor is probably going to give you a plan of action, but in case they did not or you forgot, I will tell you my advice and my rationale behind it. I tell everyone with a vomiting baby not to give their kiddo anything to eat or drink for at least two hours after they last vomited. Once they have gone two hours it is time to start slowly introducing clear liquids. Now the American Academy of Pediatrics recommends the World Health Organization's rehydration formula, the problem is this has to be made by mixing things together which are not necessarily found in every modern day kitchen these days. It is also not something available at the store (maybe I should figure out a way to package and sell it so I can be rich) and to be honest it tastes like crap. So let's assume you live here in the real world with me and eat food at restaurants, work at a real job, and do not have loads of free time to be concocting solutions to feed to your baby. I recommend unflavored Pedialyte® for the little babies less than a year of age and flavored Pedialyte® for the ones over a year of age. Pedialyte® is also available as popsicles for the older child which is a way to slowly give them fluids. In a pinch I also recommend a form of Gatorade® called G2 that has less sugar than the regular sports drink. I recommend you try to give them just a suck or two on a bottle or sippy cup every five minutes or so for the first two hours.

I like to describe a stomach virus like it makes the inside of your stomach look like a raw sore. Imagine if you skinned up your knee and it was bleeding. If you kept bending your knee it would keep bleeding, but if you were still for a couple of hours it would form a scab and stop bleeding. Now as long as you only bent your knee a little you would be fine, but if you start bending it a lot the scab will crack and start bleeding again. Now if you apply that thought process to your stomach it makes a lot more sense why you have to go real slow with pushing the fluids. Once they have held down the sips for a couple of hours then I recommend they go up to a couple ounces at a time every 30 minutes. Once they have made it six hours without vomiting then they can restart breastfeeding or formula (although I recommend changing to a lactose free formula or soy formula for about three days). The older babies can start on some bland foods and crackers. I recommend they stay away from any dairy products for three days. If they start vomiting again, start the whole process over. Typically once the vomiting has been gone for about eight hours you are usually done with it unless you give them some dairy too early.

Constipation: Constipation is hard stools that are large and painful to pass. Babies may have infrequent stooling, but if it is soft and non-painful when they do pass it, they do not have constipation. The frequency of stooling varies widely from baby to baby and from different stages of development and types of food choices. If a baby has stool that comes out in hard balls or are larger in diameter than you could imagine coming out of a baby, then it has constipation. If your baby has constipation, it is time to call your doctor. There is no one right way to treat constipation and every doctor has his or her own way of trying to control the problem. I will give you the suggestions I give parents, which maybe different from another doctor and trust me we could both be right. I tell parents once a baby gets constipated and has hard stool at the end of their intestinal tract there is nothing you can give them by mouth that is going to make stool that is already hard, come out soft. We are going to have to get the baby to get the hard stool out before we can keep them from getting hard stool again. I usually recommend a pediatric glycerin suppository inserted up their little bottom. The glycerin is just a type of grease lubricating the exit and makes it easier to pass a larger stool. Inserting the suppository also stimulates a reflex making the intestinal tract start to contract and initiate a bowel movement. I repeat the suppository every 6-8 hours until the stools are no longer hard (other doctors may recommend infant enemas which are also effective). Once the hard stool is removed some babies are done and will not get constipated again. This is often true in babies around a year of age, babies that have had a change from breastfeeding to formula, a change in formula, or a change from formula to whole milk. It is also not unusual for babies to get constipated following a diarrhea illness. If your baby is getting repeatedly constipated it is either from types of food they are eating or because they are just reabsorbing too much water out of the large intestine and making the stools dry and hard. Foods that can be constipating include bananas, cereals, peanut butter, breads, cheese and whole milk. Foods can also help clean your baby out and include your gritty fruits like prunes, pears, peaches, apples and apricots. Some babies just pull too much water out of their large intestine and have problems no matter what we add or take away from their diet. In this case your doctor may recommend adding some clear corn syrup to your baby's bottles, which has a sugar that is not so easily absorbed and pulls water into the intestine, or sometimes some medicines containing artificial sugars which do the same thing to loosen stools. Babies should never hurt when they are stooling so never accept hard painful stools as normal.

Loose Stools/Diarrhea: Trust me there is a difference between the two but you would not be able to tell it with one diaper. Both of them are very runny and thus gross. To meet the criteria for diarrhea it is a volume diagnosis. We consider any loose stools greater than six per day as diarrhea. Any number less than six per day is simple considered loose stools. Viruses, bacteria, or problems with absorption can cause diarrhea. Loose stools can be affected by fluid intake, the amount of fruit or fruit juices, the type of milk the baby eats (mainly breast milk), the normal stooling pattern (some babies always have loose stools), and even what time of year it is (we have more loose stools in the spring and fall).

We do not worry about loose stools, as they can be very normal. Diarrhea is usually nothing to worry about unless it is red or black (which can both indicate blood), lasts longer than five days, or leads to dehydration; all of these should prompt you to go see your doctor. It is not unusual for babies to get 2-3 diarrhea illnesses per year. If diarrhea lasts longer than five days or has blood in it, we worry it may be due to a bacterial infection or some process affecting absorption. It would not be uncommon for the doctor to order some test on the stool so bring the baby's last dirty diaper to the office with you (to be nice to your fellow men with noses it is best to seal it up in a zip-lock bag). For signs of dehydration, see the dehydration topic.

Blocked Tear Ducts: In medical lingo blocked tear ducts are called nasolacrimal stenosis (I usually charge at least 10 dollars for that word). It means the drain at the inside corner of each eye is blocked which causes the normal tears produced by the eye for lubrication not to drain. This blockage will cause the baby to look like they are constantly crying during the day and when they sleep will cause their eye to mat shut. It is a very common condition and is the most common reason for you to see tears in a baby who is less than two months old. Most babies will outgrow this condition and for the majority of them it goes away between two and six months of life. We usually recommend you take a soft warm washcloth and gently rub in a circular motion at the inner corner of the eye for 3-5 minutes a couple times a day. If the blockage does not resolve by the time the baby is nine months old your pediatrician will usually refer you to a pediatric ophthalmologist who will take a look at your baby and possibly recommend a surgical procedure to open up the tear duct.

Dehydration: Dehydration occurs when your balance of fluid is low. This can happen either by losing more fluid than is being taken in, or by just not taking enough fluid in to replace the amount your body is always naturally losing through urine, stool, sweat, or in your breath. For the most part it is going to happen through losses from diarrhea or vomiting more than the fluid being taken in. Signs of dehydration include decreased urination (keep track of wet diapers if your baby is sick), the inside of the mouth getting dry and tacky looking, lips getting dry (which can be peeling or all wrinkled looking), decreased tears, dry loose feeling skin (we call it tenting if you pinch the skin and it sort of just stays there in a tent appearance), or lethargy (this means just lying around and very hard to arouse). Dehydration is a very serious problem and if you believe your baby is dehydrated you need to get to your doctor's clinic or the emergency room as soon as possible.

Umbilical Hernia: To be honest, every baby will have an umbilical hernia, at least for a while. An umbilical hernia is a hole in the abdominal wall formed from where the umbilical cord goes through the abdominal wall of the baby. When the umbilical cord falls off the hole where the cord went through the abdominal wall it is called a hernia. When the baby cries or pushes out their abdomen when they are pooping you will see a bulge in their belly button. Umbilical hernias will usually close off by the time your baby is two years of age. I like to apply my "rule of thumb" in this situation; if I can put my thumb through the hole there is a good chance it is not going to go away. The umbilical hernia can bulge out quite a bit and I have seen some about the size of a peach that still go away on their own (the parents never believe me, but they do). If the umbilical hernia is still there after they are two years old then it probably is not going to go away. Most pediatric surgeons like to wait until they are between four and six years of age to fix them so the risk of putting them to sleep for the surgery goes down. This is something to ask your pediatrician, because they will know what is normally done in your area.

Chapter 21

Injuries

No Mrs. Jones we don't think you are abusing him. In fact if he didn't have at least two bruises we would think you were locking him in a cage.

The bumps, bruises, scrapes, cuts and boo-boos of childhood are the true battlefield of parenting. In the beginning it will be your job to protect them from their environment. When they learn to move you will be protecting the environment from them. Accidents will happen no matter how well you protect them. A good parent will try to minimalize injuries by good baby-proofing and close supervision. The same good parent will take care of things when all the planning falls apart and life takes over. Hopefully this chapter will help reassure you and let you know injuries happen to all children and will allow you to respond with some preparedness and knowledge. Good luck, may the scars be minimal, the healing fast and the stories be funny.

Choking: When anything except air gets in the way or goes down the airway we call the episode choking. Most of the time when a baby coughs the force of the air coming out of the lungs is enough to move whatever is in the airway out of the way. What we are worried about is when something gets stuck in the airway and coughing does not get it out. The most common cause of choking is going to be food and happens because the baby is trying to eat pieces that are too large, too much food at one time, swallow a hard piece of candy, or eat while walking and suck the food down the wrong tube when they fall. Other common objects found lodged in their throats are nuts, pins, small toys, marbles and coins. A good rule of thumb is any object that can fit through a toilet paper roll is a possible choking hazard.

A child with a choking episode may present with difficulty breathing, coughing, a weak cry or cough, cyanosis (which is a way of saying turning blue), or unconsciousness. Depending on the symptom your child is showing, the intervention you make may change. If your baby is breathing with difficulty, coughing or crying then you know they do not have a complete obstruction. Watch the baby carefully and see if they can cough the obstruction out of the airway. If the baby starts to turn blue and stop breathing then it is time to intervene and begin rescue techniques you learned in your infant CPR class. Here is a quick review of the current choking recommendations from the American Red Cross.

Infant less than one year old:

-If your baby is not able to cough up the object, ask someone to call 911 while you begin rescue treatment.

-If you are alone give two minutes of care then dial 911.

-If your baby cannot clear his airway and you believe they have an object lodged in their airway, position the baby facedown with the baby's body lying on your forearm and his head and neck supported by your hand. Lay your forearm holding the baby across your thigh for support. Try to make sure the baby's head is lower than his body. Use the heel of your free hand give five firm back blows between the shoulder blades to try to dislodge the blockage. Then with your free hand support the back of the baby's head and neck and turn the baby face up. Still keep the head lower than the body, place two or three finger tips in the midline of their chest just below their nipples and give five chest thrusts pushing down ½ to 1 inch each time.

-Continue the sequence of five back blows to five chest thrusts until the object comes out or the baby starts to cough again. If coughing let the baby try to cough up the object. If the baby stops breathing again then restart the sequence. Only pull out the object if you can see it. A blind sweep in the baby's mouth could push the object down farther into the throat.

Child older than one year of age:

-If your child is not able to cough up the object, ask someone to call 911 while you begin rescue treatment.

-If you are alone give one cycle of five back blows and five abdominal thrusts, then dial 911.

-Give five back blows using the heel of your hand between the child's shoulder blades.

-Give five abdominal thrusts (Heimlich Maneuver). Accomplish this by wrapping your arms around the child's waist, tipping them slightly forward, making a fist with one hand and placing it above the child's belly button, and with the other hand grabbing the fist and beginning quick upward thrusts toward their upper back. Look in the child's mouth for the object and if seen grab and remove.

Take a CPR class! The time you spend could very easily save your baby's life.

Fractures: Broken bones unfortunately happen in babies. The most common symptom of a fracture is going to be pain and they quit using that particular limb. The most common fractures vary depending on the age of the baby. In a newborn the most common fracture we see is a broken clavicle that often occurs in bigger babies with difficult deliveries. During the infant period fractures are going to happen most commonly when people drop them or they roll off of things. The fracture is going to vary depending on where they hit. During the toddler years the most common fractures are going to be skull fractures from falling and hitting their head, arm fractures from falling and trying to catch themselves with their arm, and finger fractures from getting their fingers slammed in doors. All suspected fractures should be seen by a doctor so the proper plan can be made to make sure the bone heals correctly and as quickly as possible. Luckily babies bones heal very fast so it will usually not have them down for long.

Head Injuries: It is a good thing skulls are made of very thick bones because babies are going to hit their heads a lot. Part of this is because their head is so big in proportion to their body, part is because they are kind of klutzy, and part is because they are little risk takers and always trying to kill themselves. There are several things to consider when they hit their head. Does their head look abnormal? Did they cut themselves and need stitches? Did they hurt their teeth or bite their tongue? Did they lose consciousness? Do they act like they know who you are and where they are? Did they start vomiting? Are they having seizures? If you answered yes to any of the questions then you need to give your doctor's office a call. Many people are worried about the size of the bruise or the amount of swelling they see. These are usually things we do not worry about and can vary depending on how many blood vessels were damaged with the injury and started to bleed. Luckily most hits to their head are going to be slight and the answer to the questions most of the time will be no. Try and reduce the amount of head injuries by baby proofing your house, wearing helmets if riding bikes, and watching them to make sure they are not trying to climb of the furniture, cabinets or drapes.

What happens if they did lose consciousness? If they passed out on impact or shortly afterward then they have suffered a concussion. A concussion can happen without losing consciousness, but definitely if they are knocked out. A concussion is a bruise to the brain and your baby will need to be evaluated by a physician immediately. A concussion can be a sign of a more serious brain injury such as a skull fracture or a bleeding blood vessel in the brain. Most concussions will be self-limited and result only in a bad headache, a scary story and a good reason to avoid head injuries.

When a person gets hit in the head and cannot remember what happened we call the condition amnesia. Amnesia is a common symptom of a concussion. The amnesia results in them not knowing who they are or where they are and is usually temporary. The amnesia to the details of the injury may be permanent. Doctors worry amnesia may be a sign a brain injury may be progressing such as a bleed in the brain.

If your baby starts vomiting after a head injury, call your doctor immediately. The most common reason for vomiting after the injury is the baby is crying so hard they make themselves throw up. Vomiting can be a sign of increased pressure on the brain occurring from swelling of the brain or from blood around or in the brain accumulating to increase the pressure.

If your baby starts to have seizures after a hit to the head, **CALL 911 IMMEDIATELY!** Your baby has a severe head injury with swelling or bleeding of the brain until proven otherwise. You will be seen immediately in the emergency department and have an emergency CT scan to determine where the injury is and what needs to be done.

If they only have a large bump it is from swelling and blood accumulating under the skin. It is best to apply pressure and ice to the bruise. Do not put ice directly onto the skin. I recommend wrapping an ice cube in a paper towel or washcloth and applying to the swelling for 3-5 minutes at a time. If the bruise is large and over the eyes or at the bridge of the nose, as the blood settles the baby may develop a black eye.

Knocked out teeth: Sad but true, sometimes a baby with those shiny white teeth takes a tumble or gets whacked and will knock out their teeth. Most of the time they are going to now be toothless until their permanent teeth come in, but before we give up hope there is some stuff to try. First take the tooth and try to shove it right back in where it came from. Sometimes it will stick in there and become tight in place again (to be completely honest I have heard this statement my entire career, but never had it work). If that did not work (you join my list of failures) drop the tooth into some milk. Now it is time to find a dentist quickly to see if they can help us out. Call the local emergency room and see if they have a dentist on call. If they do go there, if not you will want to get to a dentist's office to see if they can salvage the tooth. If they cannot, do not despair, it happens frequently and they all seem to grow up fine and the missing tooth did not cause them any long-term problems.

Lacerations: This is the fancy name for a cut. If a cut looks deep stitches may be required. So what makes a cut require stitches? We stitch up a laceration if it will not stop bleeding, if it is gaping open and looks like it would make a bad scar, or closing it up will reduce infections. If a laceration needs to be stitched up, a doctor needs to be seen right away. The longer it takes to fix the laceration the more likely it is to get infected. If a laceration is over 13 hours old most doctors will not stitch it up because of the increased risk of infection. Until you can get to the doctor try to wash the wound up thoroughly and keep pressure against the wound to reduce bleeding.

Nurse Maid's Elbow: This is a common toddler injury and will make you feel like a terrible person if it happens to your child (it is very common and you aren't necessarily a bad person...although you might be). The most common way this happens is by pulling up on your baby's hand when the weight of the baby is pulling down. This is the right mechanism to dislocate the end of the radius bone of the forearm at the elbow. Now you tell yourself this couldn't happen to you.... right? Wrong, the most common way I see it happen is you are walking with your young toddler and you are holding their hand. They decide to throw a fit and before you realize what they are doing they throw themselves to the ground. Unfortunately their hand is stationary and attached to you as their body is hurtling its way to the ground. The next thing you know your have a baby who is crying, refusing to move its arm and holding it against their chest in the position you would normally see someone hold their arm if it was in a sling. This is something you are going to need to see a doctor about because it is very easy to fix and the pain is going to stop when it gets fixed. This is one of the most satisfying things to take care of as a doctor, because when you put the bone back in place they feel completely better.

Sprains: Toddlers can sprain their ankles just like an adult and it's more likely to happen to them. Sprains can happen with falls, getting their feet stuck while walking, or going up or down stairs. Just like an adult, their ankle will swell and it will hurt. The good thing is they will heal much faster than an adult would. Apply ice and elevate the foot. Try to get them to wear shoes with more support of their ankle for the next several days. If their limp is worsening or pain is not improving after a day or two it would be a good idea to have your pediatrician take a look and make sure there is not a fracture.

Chapter 22

That really happened? Funny Stories

This chart would sure come in handy in the middle of the night to quickly fix that screaming noise coming from the nursery.

Too often we as pediatricians and parents spend too much time emphasizing how much work and how hard it is to be a parent and we lose sight of the fact children are hilarious and a great source of joy. Some of the funniest movies and television shows have revolved around what children say and do. Enjoy your baby and have fun with them. I can tell you, working with children is a fun job and has generated tons of stories and happy memories. This chapter is just in fun so do not take any of it serious as it is just a celebration of the fun taking care of children has brought to my life. This chapter contains some of the funnier phone calls, silly cures I have heard, and nonsense I have said to my patients. I hope you have learned some thing in this book and hope you will get a final chuckle out of some things in this chapter.

<u>Phone Calls:</u> (Be sure to pay attention to the time of some of these phone calls).

Time: 12:30 a.m.

Mom: "What time is our appointment in the morning?" (I did not know).

Time: 11:30 p.m. on a Saturday

Mom: "Could you go through with me again how to introduce baby food?" (I did it, but I was never quite sure why it was so important at that time).

Time: 2:30 a.m.

Mom: "Do you hear him crying? What do you think he wants?" (She obviously thought I was a better psychic than I give myself credit for being. I tried to help the best I could).

Time: 9:00 p.m.

Me: "This is Dr. James, you had me paged?"

Man: "No, I'm sure you must have the wrong number."

Me: "Is this ###-####?"

Man: "Yes."

Me: "I am a pediatrician, is there anyone there who could have needed me?"

Man: "Sir, we haven't had a child in this house for over 40 years, so either you have the wrong number or you are really slow answering your pages."

Time: 6:00 p.m. on a Friday

Dad:"Dr. James, we are leaving on vacation tomorrow. Is there anyway you could do something to make sure our baby doesn't get sick while we are gone?" (I didn't have any tricks, but I don't think they got sick).

Time: 7:30 p.m.

Me: "Hello, this is Dr. James can I help you?"

Mom: "When is it OK for a kid to drink beer?"

Me: "I believe the legal age is 21, why?"

Mom: "Would it be OK for her to drink O'douls?"

Me: "Why would you want your 18 month old to drink O'douls?"

Mom: "She loves the taste of beer."

Me: "How does she know what beer tastes like?"

Mom: "She got some of her dad's beer off the table and now she cries to have more. We thought we could give her a beer substitute."

Me: "I don't think it's a good idea to get her liking the taste of beer at 18 months of age."

Old wives' tales for cures I have heard over the years: (Not only are these not recommended, they could hurt your baby and even get them taken away from you for neglect).

Teething Pain: The most common cure for teething pain I have heard about is rubbing alcohol, usually in the form of whiskey or moonshine, on the baby's gums. The most interesting alternative I have heard is drilling a hole in a silver dime and wearing it on a necklace to prevent teething pain.

Eczema: I have had people want to rub their children down with bleach, gasoline, kerosene, and urine to help eczema. The most interesting alternative was to wear an amber crystal necklace and bracelet to prevent breakouts (a rather cool fashion statement).

Thrush: Find someone who has never seen their biological father and have them breathe into the baby's mouth to cure thrush.

Ear Pain: Pour warm urine into the baby's ear canal to soothe the pain. (Not only can I not think of a scientific reason this would work, but also it scares me to think how many urine soaked ears I may have touched).

Long Life: In order to ensure a long life a baby should fall out of bed before they are one year of age. (I have had two broken arms from baby's being pushed out of bed by their grandmother to ensure longevity).

Hivey: Much to my surprise being hivey has nothing to do with having hives. It is a fussy baby with gas. The cure is to flip their liver. This is accomplished by slowly turning the baby upside down and then rotating them back right side up. (Although the baby should be able to make this trip fairly safely if done very slow it is technically impossible for a liver to flip).

Cradle Cap: The cure for cradle cap would be putting a wet pee diaper on their head. (Yuck! Just another opportunity for me to touch pee).

Warts: In residency I was told by my attending any old wives tale we heard about would probably be about as effective as our medical treatments. My favorite cure I have heard of is to take a penny made before the year you were born, pee on the dirt, rub the penny in the mud, scratch the wart three times with the penny and then throw the penny over your left shoulder and never look back for it. (I have not done the medical study to test its effectiveness but I did like the way it sounded).

Colds: I have heard of many cures for colds, many which seem to contain alcohol, which is not good for the babies. Some of the preventive methods for colds are pretty interesting. Things like drinking a glass of orange juice everyday, eating an apple everyday, never going outside with your hair wet. My grandpa's way of preventing colds was to spend the summer outside without a shirt on. He still got some colds and has had some skin cancers removed, so I would not recommend his method.

Scrapes: Making a poultice out of chewing tobacco, dirt and birch tree bark and applying to the wound. (I guarantee it will look worse than any infection).

Splinters: Soaking your skin in a bread and milk solution or putting a piece of potato over the area with the splinter. (Starch does have a drawing property so there might be some merit to this old standard).

Colic: This one seems to always involve alcohol. I do not recommend ever giving alcohol to a baby, but giving it to the parent might be a good idea for this condition.

Pinkeye: Cured by squirting breast milk into the baby's eye. (I don't think this could hurt, but it is a little weird).

Pediatrician Brochure:
Things you should know before becoming a baby doctor

1. You will get bit. It makes sense, if you stick your finger into a wild animal's mouth it will bite you...babies...same thing applies.

2. You will get peed on even by girls; the boys you will see coming, but those girls are sneaky.

3. You will start to describe poop color and texture in terms of food.

4. You will think it's physically impossible for so much vomit and poop to come out of such a small little thing without it deflating and dying.

5. You will begin to think most doctors are complete and utter idiots.

6. You will think being a pediatrician is a job until you realize it is who you are.

7. In spite of being covered in snot, puke, pee, poop, dirt, blood, and tears you will think you have the best job ever.

8. Little kids will tell on their parents and make them turn bright red.

9. Parents will tell on themselves and make you turn bright red.

10. There are a million words to describe genitalia besides the ones you learned in medical school.

11. You will begin to believe there should be a test before a person can become a parent.

12. The best teacher you will ever have will be your own child.

13. Parents are not the enemy and many will become your dearest friends.

14. Never discount a mom's intuition; she may not know what is wrong, but she usually knows something is wrong.

15. Never forget why you went into pediatrics. The money will never be enough. The hours will never be nice enough. You will never get the respect you think you deserve. At the end of the day you get to play with kids, get hugs and pretend to never grow up while taking care of tomorrow's most precious resource…children.

Cliff James

Cliff James lives in Oak Ridge, TN with his wife Kristi, sons Dalton, Tyler and Kaden, as well as some critters. He works in a busy pediatric office and has the time of his life doing what he knows he was meant to do…take care of children. He is the founder of www.pedvaccines.com and is currently working on a new website www.helpmommy.com which will be launching in 2016.

My story started September 30, 1969. I remember it being a warm, sleepy experience when I was suddenly awoken to bright lights, loud noises, and someone smacking me on my bootie. It was then that I realized I was naked as a jaybird and have had a fear of public nudity ever since. Some guy with one foot in the grave was holding me by one foot and I saw a smiling tired lady with long, dark hair and a dude with a silly smile standing next to her. I guess they didn't know what to call me so they just started calling me the same thing the guy with the silly smile was called and just slapped another number at the end of the name.

I grew up in the country in the middle of nowhere surrounded by children, not because there were lots of people out there, but because the tired lady and the guy with the silly smile thought they should have a whole lot of kids. For some reason all of the kids they had except me were deformed little boys that were missing some parts, so we called them sisters. My dad, the guy with the silly smile, was a hard worker, mom was making a home (something like that) and five kids were making a lot of messes and a bunch of noise

My grandma told me that I was going to grow up and become a pediatrician and it seemed like a good idea. I attended West Texas State University and got a degree in biology. With this degree you are given the choice of going to school or starving to death so off to medical school I went. I started medical school at Texas Tech Health Science Center in Lubbock, TX. Somehow I managed to survive and thrive in medical school in spite of violating all the dress codes and all known stereotypes of medical students. When I finished medical school it was painfully obvious that I was still an idiot so I moved on to the next step of becoming a pediatrician and went to Cleveland, OH and spent three years as an indentured servant, but learned a whole lot about pediatrics.

In July of 2000 I started practicing in Oak Ridge, TN

Dan Rosandich

Illustrator Dan Rosandich is a fulltime cartoonist and has been publishing cartoons for 40 years. His cartoons have appeared in magazines such as Saturday Evening Post, Reader's Digest, Barrons and Woman's World. Many of his panels have appeared in the New York Times Best Selling series Chicken Soup For The Soul including: The Mother's Soul, The Christian Soul, The Pet Lover's Soul, and many others. Dan offers thousands of his cartoons to license for many applications including newsletters, presentations, and web usage. Images can be easily downloaded for specific uses and visit www.DansCartoons.com <http://www.DansCartoons.com> for more information. Dan specializes in "custom cartoons" like those created for this book and can assist anyone with a specific project that needs to be illustrated. He can easily be reached via his web catalog page.

CPSIA information can be obtained
at www.ICGtesting.com
Printed in the USA
LVOW01s2249110117
520622LV00004B/5/P